I0583167

Flying South
No. 5
2018

Managing Editor: Steve Lindahl

Poetry Editor: Angell Caudill

Non-fiction Editor: Jennifer Stevenson Vincent

Fiction Editor: Ray Morrison

Fiction Readers: Bob Shar
                     Steve Lindahl

President's Favorite chosen by:
                     Bart Ganzert

Cover Art: Barbara Rizza Mellin

Flying South is a literary magazine/writing contest published annually by Winston-Salem Writers, an association of writers and readers with the purpose of:

Helping writers interact with other writers, improve their craft, and realize their goals.

Information about Winston-Salem Writers can be found at the website: **www.wswriters.org**

Winston-Salem Writers is a non-profit organization and a member of The Arts Council of Winston-Salem and Forsyth County, NC.

Contents

2018 Best in Category Winners:

Non-Fiction:

Fiction:

Poetry:

Spencer K. M. Brown

Water in a Sieve

The snow fell for four days without stopping and the land looked pale and lonesome out of his window. His toes had gone numb sometime during the night and he paused as he stood up out of bed. He made a little fist with one foot, the other, summoning the warm lifeblood back into them. His brother Henry was still sleeping and he had a brief thought of not waking him, but ignored it, snatching off all of the blankets at once, revealing the skinny, pale figure which shriveled fetally like a worm that had just been poked with a stick. There was a frozen moaning from Henry, followed by words that were cut silent as Levi closed the door behind him.

His mother was just beginning to get a fire going in the living room as he came down the stairs. The house was cold and held a certain emptiness in the air, one that did not feel like home, not his home, but rather some wintering version of it. Levi and his brother stopped asking about the heat after a few weeks. Everyday their father would say someone would be coming out that next day to take a look at things, but no one ever showed up the next day. Levi knew what he meant to say. Someone would come when they could afford it, when things got a little easier for them. But things were the same. They always were the same and would be. Someone would come when his father could work more hours and save a little extra for things like fixing the furnace. But by the time that could happen, there would be no need for heat anymore.

Levi opened the oven and took his pair of socks out, leaving his brother's pair on the rack to keep warm. He sat at the table and pulled them on, coughing suddenly as plumes of gray smoke filled his lungs.

Gotta open the flue, Ma, he said, hiding his face in the collar of his shirt.

I did. Air just needs to catch hold of it, she said.

There any breakfast?

Hold on, I'll fix you somethin.

His mother came into the kitchen wiping the soot off her hands with her red apron. She brought him a cup of coffee and he drank, staring out through the back windows. Everything seemed shapeless, melted and dried stiff into a frozen twist of branches and felled trees. She brought him a plate of fried eggs and biscuits left over from dinner the night before.

Is your brother ever gettin up? she said.

I woke him, he said.

Levi felt the cold air whispering on his bare skin where his clothes didn't quite cover. It would be a few months still before he would get Henry's next hand-me-downs. He chewed and set his fork down, resting his hands on the hot mug.

Where's Dad?

He ain't home yet, his mother said. Had to go out in the middle of the night. Someone called in again.

Well, that's good for us, ain't it?

I suppose it's somethin, she said. She paused at the sink and gazed distractedly out the window at the blankness of everything. Levi watched her as he ate, suddenly feeling like he should say something. But what was there to say? It used to be that he could talk about anything with his mother. Just chat away the mornings about anything at all. Something had changed. Levi, it might have been Levi who changed. He was not a little boy anymore, not just a simpleminded boy; he was becoming a man. As he watched her, he knew that she hadn't changed. She was still his mother. Still the same beauty his father loved and continued to love. A face more tired, perhaps. The youthful glaze that had once been now dulled and slipping away like water in a sieve, all of it passing and only the hardened version of things remaining. Perhaps nothing had changed at all. Perhaps it had always been like this, only, he saw things for what they actually were now. No change at all except for a balance. One thing dying so another can bloom. He thought about this, about these things, as he ate and stared out into the same nothingness as his mother.

Have you fed Brutus? Levi asked.

I put food out for him but haven't seen him. Must be out in the yard.

Levi took a last bite of his food that had now gone cold, the yolks stiff and the biscuit staling faster than his appetite. His mother cleared his dishes, refilled the coffee, and set a plate out for Henry as she heard him coming down the stairs. Henry hit Levi on the back of the head as he passed, then got his socks out of the oven.

You little jerk, Henry said, staring at Levi across the table.

Have to get up earlier, Levi said.

I'll kick your ass little boy.

Henry Wafford Post, their mother snapped. That tongue of yours will be your ruin. Apologize to him.

Henry looked at her, then back at his little brother.

Right this minute, she said.

I'm sorry, little boy, he said and then began shoveling in his breakfast.

I need your boys' help today, she said. We have to get this house in order before tonight.

What's tonight? Henry said, a spray of dried biscuit crumbs raining over the table.

We're havin the Bishops over for dinner.

I can't, Henry said. I told Maggie I would have dinner at her house tonight.

Well, that was a stupid thing to do, she said. Because now you'll have to cancel.

But Ma, the Bishops are your friends. They ain't mine.

You're not goin anywhere tonight, understood?

Levi smiled at his brother. He watched Henry's lips mouth the words FUCK YOU at him, and he just smiled wider.

Where's Brutus at? Henry said.

Out in the yard, Levi said.

He needs to eat. Has he eaten, Ma?

No, not yet.

He's sick, Henry said, turning in his chair to look out the back windows at the yard. He needs to eat, Ma.

Well, go and get him in here then.

Who let him out? He ain't supposed to go out. I told you all that. He's sick.

He's always sick though, Levi said.

Yes, he always sick, Henry said. Brutus is a sick dog, that's why I take care of him. He will always be sick.

Why would you keep a sick dog? Levi said.

Brutus is loyal. And no matter how sick, you don't just forget somethin like that.

All I know is that that dog has costed you an arm and both legs takin care of him, their mother said.

He's a good hunter, that's why, Henry said. Dad picked him out himself. And he'll be a good hunter again. You'll see.

He's sick though, Levi said.

Sometimes things get sick, sometimes they don't. He's sick right now but he'll get better. You just wait and see.

You boys wanna go up town for me?

If it gets me out of here, Henry said.

I only need a few things for tonight, she said and sat to write a list for them.

Can I go? Levi said.

No.

Yes, you can, their mother said.

You really think the Bishops wanna have dinner in the damn arctic circle? Henry said.

Your Daddy's gonna get it fixed this afternoon he said. One way or another.

He ain't gonna fix shit, Henry whispered to his brother.

Here's twenty dollars, she said. I want change and a receipt, you got it? Every penny, Henry.

All right, all right, he said, stuffing the money in his pocket. He ate the last bites of his breakfast as he walked his plate over to the sink. He wiped his mouth on his shirttail and headed for the door, his little brother chasing after him.

Can you keep an eye out for Brutus? Henry said. He needs to eat, Ma.

I will, she said. Be back quick. Got it? I need your boys' help today, I mean it.

Henry opened the door, pushing Levi out of the way, then ran out the door and down the driveway. Levi raced down the porch and out into the snow, catching up with Henry.

What all do we need to get?

Don't matter, Henry said. I'm in control of the list.

The two of them walked, listening to the crunch of snow beneath their boots, Levi a few steps behind his brother. The sky was heavy and swollen and running like watered ink but the snow had stopped for the morning. Everything was pale and illuminated in a blanket of white. They were silent for a time as they made their way up the hill that cut through a pasture and led to town. There were no cars on the roads and most of the roads had still not been plowed. Levi looked far down the stretch of white road ahead of them and wondered where their father might be at that moment. Sitting in the little draughty cab of the truck. Plowing the curving mountain roads. Alone and silent among the drifts of snow.

Levi had only recently started to worry about his father after he overheard his parents talking late one night about how his father had had to help a coworker. The man's plow had slid off the road and broken through the guardrail down the highway near Bull Mountain. The truck tumbled and turned end over end and all the way down into the valley. The driver broke his neck and was dead and gone by the time Levi's father had found him. He carried his body all the way back up the hill and to the main road. Lots of folks ran off the roads in the winter, his father had said. Levi prayed that his father would never be one of them.

You think Dad will ever die? Levi said.

That's the dumbest thing I ever heard you say, Henry said. Of course he will. Everyone will.

When do you think?

Who knows. Could be tomorrow, could be another fifty years. Hell, he might be dead this minute for all we know.

Don't say that.

It's the truth. Who knows though. Who knows, who cares?

Think he'll go to heaven?

Dad? Yeah. He's a hard worker. Honest. Brave. He'll be up there all right.

What about me? Levi asked.

Well, the verdict's still out on you. Gotta work hard for somethin like eternity. Never just assume.

What about you?

Yep, I'll go.

Ma says you cuss too much though.

Hell, the Lord knows it's just frustration. He don't care any which way about cussin. It's what you do that matters, not what you say.

By the time the boys got back to the house their mother was on hands and knees scrubbing the floors in the kitchen. Her hair tied up in a silky flower-patterned scarf. The house had warmed a little and the smell of the fire made Levi feel safe.

Change and receipt, their mother said, not stopping her work as they came in. And take your shoes off.

I know, I know. Henry set the grocery bags on the counter.

I want you both to start with the bathroom, she said. And then we need to figure out how to rearrange that dining room.

Dad home? Levi asked.

Not yet, she said. He called earlier, said he's picking up an extra route. He won't be home until late. She paused, wiping her brow, kneeling and looking silently out the window.

You feed Brutus? Henry said.

Haven't seen him, she said, coming back to her work.

Goddamn, still?

Watch your mouth, Henry, she said.

He needs to eat, Ma, I told you that.

He'll come eat when he's ready. He always does.

Not when he's sick. He don't know what to do when he's sick.

What do you want me to say, Henry. She stood, rinsing out the rags and dumping the dirty water down the sink.

I need to go find him.

You need to do what I told you and start helpin me.

Let me just go and find him first, please.

Fine, go and get him, she said, shaking her head. But hurry, all right? I really need your help. I mean it.

Henry went to the back door and Levi followed.

You put that change on the counter? their mother said.

Henry stopped in his tracks and came back into the house, reluctantly putting the change beside the bags.

You hurry, I mean it, she said.

The boys walked off the porch and into the backyard. The ground was perfectly flat and smooth, with only a random sapling or branch sticking up through the snow. The boys stood looking all around them for the dog. Levi felt the cold air deep in his lungs and watched the smoke as he exhaled. The heavy sky darkened the world around them bringing a lonesome air to the forest which surrounded.

Brutus! Henry called out through his gloved hands.

There's his paw tracks over there, Levi said.

They ran up to the tracks and started following them into the woods, one on either side.

Poor bastard, Henry said. Probably went out and got lost.

They walked quickly along the jagged paw prints that curved through the woods among the trees. The forest was silent and there was only the sound of their footfalls. The forest was bare and a great blur of browns and grays shot up among the drifts of white. The underbrush was dead and buried beneath the winter. The cold surrounded them, it bit at their lips and made their noses run endlessly. Levi could feel his feet sweating inside his boots. They were both hot and frozen all at once. Henry took off his knit cap and brushed his hands through the sweaty mess of dirty blond hair. The tracks went light for a moment and they stopped just at the top of a slope which led down into a deep holler.

You see where they went?

Levi looked around on the ground, taking a few steps down the slope.

Found them, he said, pointing.

The boys walked with sideways steps down the slope. The air felt colder suddenly and a breeze pushed through the woods.

Stop that, Henry said. Just stop.

I'm not doin nothin, Levi said.

Not you, the wind. You have to talk to it.

The wind can't hear you.

Sure it can. Everything can hear us. Just because it can't talk doesn't mean it can't listen.

Where'd you hear that? Levi said. He took a bad step and slipped, falling to the ground and sliding a several yards down to the bottom of the holler.

Serves you right for doubting me, Henry said. He helped his brother to his feet. Dad told me that, though. He said everything is a reflection of the Lord. And the Lord can hear our prayers, so why can't all his creations hear, too?

Levi looked at his brother a moment. So trees can hear us?

he said.

Bet your sweet ass they can.

I don't see how. They ain't even got ears.

Not like us they don't, but they can hear. Indians believed it, too.

They came to a creek which cut through the holler like a long white serpent. The parts where snow had not fallen babbled with a weak pulse of water.

They jumped across the creek and looked around for where the tracks picked up again. Levi looked skyward as he felt snow falling.

I think it's snowin again, he said.

No, just the wind knocking it out of the trees, Henry said. Here, I found them. Brutus! Brutus!

Brutus! Levi called out. He felt more snow on his head and brushed it off his face. No, it's snowin. It is.

Goddamn, Henry said. We have to hurry or it'll cover up the tracks. Brutus!

They followed the paws up the back side of the slope, angling out towards a meadow on the other side of the forest. They started to walk faster as the snow fell harder. They raced up the hillside and out to the line of trees where forest turned into meadow. The wheat was tall, nearly to their waists, and thin in winter and they followed the tracks to the edge of it. Looking out at the landscape ahead of them, everything was a blur of white as the levee of clouds broke and let the snow fall.

I can't see the tracks, Levi said.

Brutus!

What are we gonna do?

Brutus! Come on boy. Brutus!

Henry.

Would you shut up, Henry said. We're gonna walk all through the grass until we find them again.

He could be anywhere though.

Well, you best start lookin then. He put his hands around his mouth, taking a deep, painful breath and called out, Brutus!

The boys stood on the edge of the tree line. Levi watched the snow fall in thick flakes, effortlessly slaloming though the frozen air.

Quit daydreamin, Henry said. You start lookin that way and I'll go over here. Really look for them.

Levi walked with his head bent down, listening to his brother's voice echoing out across the hills. He held his eyes on the ground watching the stalks of wheat pass by like trees on the highway. Everything was slowly becoming more and more white. His toes were beginning to itch as they went cold and warm all at once. He ran in quick bursts through the grass, looking up every few steps to see where his brother was. He saw a few tracks suddenly and widened his eyes in the harsh glare of snow.

I see them, Henry, I see them! He raced through the grass following the tracks. Henry! he called out. He followed them and they were getting lighter and lighter with each second of snow fall. He ran quicker until he was suddenly beside his brother.

Did you hear me, I found the tracks again, he said. As he looked at his brother, he became silent. Henry stood there motionless in the snow, the wind moved tall grass and it brushed against his flannel coat. Levi followed his brother's stunned gaze and saw Brutus lying there on the cold earth. His tongue stiff and hanging out of his open mouth in a great sleep. His brown fur slowly gathered the snowflakes and frost had sealed his eyes closed.

Neither of the boys said anything for several moments. They simply stood, staring down at the dead dog as the snow fell sideways in the wind. Henry sniffed the clear drips of snot back into his nose. Levi watched his face shift from sorrow to anger and back again.

Is he dead? Levi whispered.

Of course he's dead, dipshit, Henry said.

Well should we just leave him here?

No, Henry said, bending down. He put his hands on the cold, stiff fur, petting the creature as he had done a thousand times before.

Well, what are we gonna do?

We're gonna take him home.

But what'll Ma say? She don't want him in the house.

Henry reached out and gathered his dog into his arms. Clumps of snow fell of its fur and dropped to the ground. As he stood he started to walk off back towards the woods and Levi looked down at the perfect outline of Brutus that remained in the snow. The snow fell, slowly filling the place where the dog had laid, slowly washing away the moment.

Levi walked a few steps behind his brother, saying nothing, listening to the snow which surrounded him. He could hear his brother crying as he carried the dog across the creek and into the holler. The smell of chimneys and fire creeping through the forest just behind him. Levi looked around at the trees, at the saplings which poked up out of the earth, struggling to feel the gray sunlight. He wondered if the trees were listening now. He listened to the forest listening to the sound of his wet boots trudging through the snow.

Henry? Levi said as they reached the top of the slope.

Yeah.

Where is Brutus now?

I don't know.

He was good though, wasn't he?

Yeah.

So he would go to heaven, too.

No, it don't work like that.

So he's just nowhere?

I don't know.

Levi looked at the bareness of the forest around him. Through the trees and falling snow he could see their house coming into site like a photograph developing. He watched his brother carrying the dog in his arms and listened to everything around him. He felt the cold air cut down into his lungs and felt his toes going numb again. He hoped his father would be home by the time they got there.

He felt the winter breathe down upon his skin where his coat didn't quite cover and said nothing at all. He felt his words moving out in small breaths through the forest and off into the hills. He felt something shifting its shape around him, within him. Something had changed and yet was exactly the same. The snow fell and suddenly lightened and was gone as they came through the woods.

We gotta hurry, Henry said, turning to wait for his brother to catch up. Levi looked at the scars of tears which had frozen on his brother's cheeks. Mom needs our help.

Will she be mad we were gone so long?

No, she won't.

The boys walked side by side all the way back to the house.

The warmth wrapped around Levi as he stepped inside. He stood in the kitchen a moment, watching his brother lay the dog down in the snow, kneeling beside it. He watched and listened to the silence from the doorway. The wind stopped and the snow stopped and he wondered if the trees were listening to Henry as he whispered something to Brutus. Where was Brutus now, where was his father. Where was he? And he stood there feeling himself push off through time and out through the hills in great breaths. He listened to the trees listening and felt the winter move through time for a hundred years. He watched as Henry knelt and ran his hands across the dog's soft fur for the last time, just as he had done a thousand times before.

Allen Guest

An Order Obtains

These days I am not
much concerned with
the order of things – the sequencing,
the ranking, the one two
three four
of this thing and
that thing,
and of people, too.
It seems an unknowable
order obtains over
any observation
or objection
I might make.

A season of winter follows
that of fall, just as darkness follows dusk.
But given time, each comes around again,
and what was first is now
equally second, and
second first, and declaring
a proper order is clear folly, as if one were
judging the winner of the horse race on
the merry-go-round at the county fair.

I offer this: the horse's saddle.
Consider its middle point.
Running longways, that is from
head-to-tail on the horse, the midpoint is

a low point, a valley if you will.
But run shortways, that is from
stirrup to stirrup, that same point is
a high point, a peak if you will.
That is the most order we can make
of it – every low place also a high, and
every high as well a low.

Contentment is to run as horses on
the merry-go-round, each of us
simultaneously first and last, gently
bobbing up and down, all the while
hearing organ music, fireworks, laughter,
smelling popcorn, and feeling
the heels of children spur
us along, racing in circular moonlight with
a cool October breeze in our manes.

Elizabeth Crowell

War and Peace

I have Stage IV cancer. I will probably not have time to read the books in my own house, not to mention the other books that I intended to read or that have yet to be written. I meant to read much more, of course, all the time, since my earliest days when I checked out four library books for every one I read. *War and Peace* is a book that has remained with me my adult life, like an aunt in Ohio I never met but whom I really plan to visit at some point.

My failure to read *War and Peace* is vivid because of the way the book was introduced to me. I took a course in college called General Literature, a survey of world literature that started with *The Iliad* and ended with (you guessed it!) *War and Peace*. I have a memory that I read every book before *War and Peace*, except for say, the second half of *Don Quixote*, but, if quizzed about any of the titles now, (*The Divine Comedy*, all of it, *Gargantua and Pantagruel*, *The Tempest*, *Anthony and Cleopatra*, *The Aeneid*, etc.) I would fail utterly. Of course, this is one of the mysteries of reading, that out of what is vivid at the time, only a few details remain.

The professor of this class was a man who had a first name that rhymed with his last name. He wore bell-bottomed jeans and a loose-fitting shirt with a half-smoked pack of cigarettes in the pocket. He had crinkled, long hair and wire-rim glasses. He looked like a heroin dealer on a 1970's TV show.

We slouched in our seats, in preppy sweaters with anchors or sailboats on them, thick duck shoes, and bright argyle socks. We spent our vacations from our all-women's and very feminist college earning money to try to look like pictures from *The Preppy Handbook*. We thought we were suffering through something.

I remember the professor as horribly boring, but I suspect that is not the case at all. I suspect my mind was washed by these incredible brownies that were often served at lunch, which were called dream bars, and set us in a haze of God-knows what, making the fairly intelligent thoughts of this sweet man absolutely impossible to reach. If I found him dull, he found me the same. He wrote such things as "ee-gads" on my papers and "that is a grotesque splitting of an infinitive!"

There was one aspect of this professor that fascinated me and perhaps it is because my own life is more tenuous than ever, that I have thought again of him. He had tried to kill himself, and in the crease of his forehead there was a messy scar, proof of his failed attempt. Because I had read so lightly and rarely listened in class, I spent considerable time thinking about what it might have felt like to have decided to end one's life, to have failed at that, and to go on and to teach entitled preppies from Connecticut books they rarely bothered to read. Given the number of purposeful deaths in *The Iliad, The Aeneid and The Divine Comedy*, it gave me great things to ponder. How could one want to do away with one's life? How could one try? How could one fail? The rumor was he had done it over a girl, and that was verified years later by a legitimate source, a chain-smoking professor. Such romance and tragedy happened in all the great books, but for me, age twenty, this professor's sad past and his resolution of it (evidently, for here he was!) held some power, and, indeed, through the years and during this difficult illness I have contemplated his scar, his badge of survival and despair. I don't know why, given the thirty years of other life experiences, I should land back at the view of his forehead more than once. When I was told my diagnosis, I thought of asking my oncologist this very question: "Should I start reading *War and Peace* now or later?" In other words, how much time do I have?

The professor, having died (of a heart attack, how fitting), could not have known of, nor can I tell him now, how exactly the picture of him came back to me as I rested from chemo, how clearly he and his advice returned.

One spring afternoon, he leaned on his podium, his scar gleaming in the sun that came through the high windows of the classic, academic building. The daffodils were out; we were all falling in or out of love. His words were not apt to do any good, but he went on bravely. If you are going to read *War and Peace*, he said, you must take some rolls of Ritz crackers and a jar of peanut butter and go to the library. (Of course, eating in the library was strictly forbidden.) Find a comfy chair, he advised. Sit there for a few days and read the whole book from beginning to end.

I meant to do exactly that. I can't imagine where those days went, where so many days have gone when I could have read *War and Peace*.

I don't want to die soon. I mean, I know that sounds obvious, and I know it is some sickness of the soul, some misappropriated notion that caused that professor to attempt to end it all. I know that almost all of literature is about the soul's inability to get it right and about the incredible limits of the body.

While I wish I could end the piece with the fact that I have read *War and Peace*, that it was enormously satisfying, that the way the words floated off the page made 19th century Russia come to life, that I am now ready to die. I can only tell you this. It is on my bedside stand. I might get to it.

David Dixon

LAS TRES MARIAS

sometimes when you die
you grow so big
so fast
that you find you
must hurry
to reach down
between your toes
and retrieve
your lucky star

it's a keepsake
a token of affection
and esteem
the one thing
you do get to take
and the very least
the gods could do

and other times
when you die
you become so small
so slowly
that one day all
that remains
and all we can find
and all that truthfully
matters
is the gradual loss of Orion
in a southern sky

and so we sit at twilight
programs in hand
waiting for the empty
black hole of a curtain
to rise

as if there were
some celestial map
as if we could
expect a guide

to each of our
un-twinklings

Donna Love Wallace

I WANT YOU TO KNOW

— to an unborn grandchild

I want you to know hydrangea's globes,
     how they nod agreement with prevailing breeze.
One flowery head rests on a stone, waiting for fire,
     eyeing dry logs stacked there.

I want you to know the dense birch canopy writhes in wind,
     rhythms her limbs like a Bengalese dancer,
know the way a hummingbird at rest resembles one leaf,
     soon leaves on opal wings.

How the caterpillar casts its hanging home, not knowing
     if it will grow or escape, its glass-
paned wings unfold, circle the fermenting fruit,
     how every hungry bird watches this.

Claire Thomas

Marfa Lights

The sun casts its cruel heat onto the black asphalt. I imagined the road as a graveyard paved with the melted tires of ignorant drivers as I began my descent into town. I was in a fold of the Chinati Mountains in remote West Texas. Here the mountains were jagged and unusual, like driving past sideways. The sign on the side of the road read "Marfa".

I had rented a room from a woman named Renee who named her garage-turned-apartment Chez Renee. The apartment sat adjacent to her home at the end of a dusty back alley. It was small, but clean and sprinkled with personal touches. I took note of an old AM antenna radio and percolator that sat on the desk in the bedroom as she walked me through. She directed me to the window and, reaching for the wooden planks sitting on each side, demonstrated how to prop the windows open. Renee assured me I would like the cool desert breeze come nightfall. The bathroom had double doors that lead outside while a ceramic clawfoot tub sat in the center. She explained it was her mother's tub from Kansas and how very difficult it was to transport. "You've both travelled a long way to be here".

It was my fifth day on the road and I was relieved to be done with the day's drive. The sun was setting and the chill was beginning to settle over the town. Outside of the windows the dry shrubs poked up across the dusty alleyways and yards casting their silhouettes before the half-light. I turned the squeaky faucet and, within an hour of my arrival, I was bathing in Renee's mother's tub from Kansas. While soaking, I read a book found on the bedroom shelf titled "Tales of the Big Bend." A chapter on the Marfa Lights was listed in the table of contents and I turned the pages accordingly. The piece of sky I could see through the double doors turned a deep black color and I unplugged the stopper. Once clean from the day's 500-mile drive, I walked out to my car with my keychain flashlight aimed at my feet to watch for rattlesnakes. With high beams on, I backed out from the side of Chez Renee and drove to the outskirts of the dusty, sleepy town.

The Marfa lights viewing area sat off of the highway that somehow seemed more deserted than it had earlier that day. The night was so dark that the light from my car stereo was glaring in contrast and my headlights were absorbed by the black void right outside of my window. Lamp posts lit the walkway to the viewing area platform and I took a deep breath of relief. The platform was a concrete slab, perfectly perched for gazing out onto the vast West Texas plateau. The Chinati mountains loomed like ghosts in the distance as the peaks appeared dark against an even darker sky.

I remembered the chapter in "Tales of the Big Bend" which discussed the mysterious Marfa lights and the ghosts which haunted the foothills that stretched in front of me. The lights had never been explained and fables surrounding this phenomenon were boundless. Ghosts of settlers, cowboys and Native Americans were thought to float around this part of the desert, sometimes manifesting as floating orb-like lights, which would later be named the Marfa Lights. According to the book, WWII-era Marfa had an Air Force base. One night, during a test run, pilots mistook these lights for a landing strip and crashed the plane into the hills. Shortly after the accident, the base was abandoned. Still it sits in this forsaken corner of West Texas as the pilots continue to float through the hills, searching for a place to land.

As I looked to the hills, the Marfa lights looked like headlights, as Renee told me they would. But, unlike headlights, they didn't flicker or dwindle but remained still and gave off a steady stream of light from miles away. I stood there staring at them for a while. The longer I did, the less I understood them. I thought of the next day's drive and how, at that time tomorrow, I would be rolling into Flagstaff, Arizona, two states over. The strangeness of the thought surged through me and I was terrified. The seclusion of West Texas made me feel further away from anything I ever had before, yet, by the end of the week, I would be arriving in California with nothing but the clothes in my car, one friend waiting on me and no road left to drive.

I got back into my car and, kicking up clouds of dust, made my descent back into town. I was to be 600 miles west of Marfa by the next evening, the thought draining my body of all remaining energy, and I was looking forward to sleep. Hopefully I would find a similar, guiding light in California, I thought. Hopefully, then, I would find my place to land.

Jenny Bates

Schopenhauer's Heart

Why was I not made of stone like thee?

- Victor Hugo

Mud dauber wasps drill
new hearts into mummified spiders.

Hoarse Goldfinches whir disapproving
mantras into the hearts of Blue Jays

defiant where not wanted,
they know their weapons

are greater than those around them.
It is a big forest, they will negotiate.

My finger parleys comfortably
in the stone hearts dip at the top.

I avoid the sharpness at the bottom.
It is a union I collect

as I go along in a wood
devoid of flattering mirrors,

broken altars always the same shape
arranged, tended, a tortured

conclave artfully settled, waiting
for a new star to be found.

You live in their presence
these bargain stones but

they are not yours. No alchemy
can make them beat your rhythm.

They lay rowed like Spirits
in a rudderless boat

pulled from living rocks
by a Mayan priest - an empty

egg stolen from a tree.
My finger loves touching them

imagining they were once
traveled by you.

Joanne Durham

The Field

"Psychedelic therapy, whether for the treatment of psychological problems or as a means of facilitating self-exploration and spiritual growth, is undergoing a renaissance in America." – Michael Pollan, NY Times Magazine, May 20, 2018

         Envision yourself in a field,
         intones my yoga teacher.
Just   like   that
         I'm back fifty years to a sun-soaked
                morning
after dropping
    acid,
        found ourselves   in a meadow
    in rural Virginia, not knowing
        or caring

        where we were

        Three women,
    wandering
        into wildflowers   and   seedlings
          of summer grass, danced
    to the harmony
        of dandelions and bees,
took off
    our shirts
        and lay
        in soft
          abundance,
                loving every tiny

moving molecule   of our own bodies,
      awake   and   true,   and   then

a distant   figure   approaching,
a man in well-worn overalls with a shotgun,
        Get out of here, get off my land,

   and calmly   with smiles
      embracing him, no thought
        of fear
          or anger
            or loss,   we pulled our shirts
back over our heads
        and took his meadow with us as we left.

Here again, it surrounds me,
      the landscape of my half moons
         and   peaceful   warriors,
    body and space one stream of energy,
      fingertips
        becoming
          the air
           they touch.

     When my teacher says,
lift your gaze, trust your strong legs to hold you,

I do. Because once I found
        myself
    in a field   of endless   possibilities,
      so I know
        exactly
         what
          she means.

JoAnn Hoffman

Desert Benediction

The concrete hall is long and low,
no stained glass here to catch the glow
and slant of morning sun. The walls,
stark white. The hopeful pews, grim rows

of metal chairs. No mellow bell calls
worshippers to prayer. The nakedness appalls
us. Still, some ancient longing draws
us here like monks approaching choir stalls.

Stranded in this desert space, we pause
to chant our praise and need, the laws
of separate faith dissolving into one.
An acolyte ignites the flame to cause

the incense to arise and stun
our senses with a cloud of scent that none
denies is blessing won.
One fragrant invocation,
one primal longing. One.

Mason Rizzo

Three Hundred Seventy-Five Degrees

The oven wailed its sirens of completion
as county paramedics whispered prayer over papa –
it's probably routine, this layer of communion
between ghost white body and off-white sheet.

The quail he'd killed and cleaned last Sunday was still roasting
hissss-spatter-pop when the old man dropped
surrounded by the untidiness of life's work –
chopped cabbage in the mixing bowl, mayo jar open,

sweating beside the sugar sack. My papa howled out to god
but that was momma who caught him on the fall –
probably dead before he hit the ground was our condolence and that may
      be,
but he was warm when I kissed his head, something like goodbye on
      my lips

but I could only think that this summer will swelter.

Phyllistine Poole

The Root Worker

"I could tell it was you by your lil' cute walk," the old man said after she got in.

Almost always Juanita turned down rides to school with men who always seemed to be around to give a young girl a ride—especially one like Juanita, shapely slim, the color of caramel.

But she knew this man and thought he was safe because he was old—had sons with children in high school with her, and some older. But it was hard to see wrinkles in the black skin, deepened and toughened by a lot of living and cunning and surviving. She could see the strength in his efficient-looking body: little and hard. Even the scruffy hair was tough, mostly black, still holding off the gray.

"You didn't know who I was at first," he said, looking in the rear-view mirror and pulling away from the curb. "You used to seeing me in my pick-up. Drive it when I'm working. Folks don't like to see me coming to their houses to work in big new cars."

They exchanged dry almost-smiles at his concession to making a living. He was a brick mason. Juanita knew him because he had built a new porch for her mother.

The big shiny yellow car slowly took them past scenery that made her feel good, and, as she glanced out of the window, he took a look at her thigh where the stylishly short, pink and white striped dress fell short, especially when she sat down.

She saw a line of little wood-frame houses in faded blues and grays. In their yards, lots of bright, frilly, carefully grown spring flowers sweetened the air. On her way home from school, she would see people, glad to be home from work, in these yards and on these porches. Now the porches and streets were empty because it was late morning. She was late for school.

"How's your mama?" Mr. Barnes was asking. Juanita turned back to his smile and answered that her mother was all right. "Miz Miller's a mighty fine woman," he said reverently. Then silence. Looked as if something was on the old man's mind. He looked as if he's suddenly seen something. His eyes pinpointed her face.

"You a fall child. I can tell. Let's see...You was born around the last of October or the first of November. That right?"

"October 31," she told him.

His head bobbed softly and he smiled. "I could tell. Special people, fall children. Lots of wisdom in fall children. I could tell you was a fall child."

She remembered, one of the neighbors said Mr. Barnes could work roots.

"I can tell things," he said. "Was born with powers to see things. " Frequently, his eyes paused from the road to look at her. She didn't like his eyes. She had known they were strange, had thought they were gray; but this close, she was a little startled to see that they were blue—alien in the face the color of tree bark—blue like frothy waters of the Atlantic Ocean she had seen whipped against the shore of the beach. She began to feel the way she did near bodies of water: aware that the promise of danger flowed in waters. Juanita was self-consciously aware of his blue glances. Infrequently, she glanced back as he talked, but most of the time she looked over the dashboard at the road ahead.

They had turned down a street of old-fashioned two-story houses.

"I used to go with a woman live back there in that house," he said nodding toward a house on the right. "Used to blow three times when I went by her house and go wait for her in the parking lot behind the club up the street. You mighta seen her: big hipped, high yellar woman. Got red, red hair settin' on top of her head like a ball of fire.

Juanita didn't remember having seen the woman.

"Anything she needed, I got. I always been good that way. "Wife say she feel like having some fish, and I got a freezer full of meat, but I go get her some fish. I likes to see people get what they wants and helps 'em if they needs it."

He smiled impishly. The blue eyes shimmered. "Over at the school sometimes, I send word that I'm outside behind the auditorium; girls come to meet me. I take 'em downtown and buy 'em whatever they want."

Juanita didn't return his smile. She wished he would drive a little faster.

"Money ain't no problem, he said, leaning to one side so that one hip lifted off the seat a little. His free hand dug into the hip pocket of everyday pants of a dark dull blue, a shade darker than his shirt. He pulled out a little brown book. Juanita saw the bulging veins traveling the hand. Wobbling fingers, buckled and curved like tree roots, managed to open the savings book, and he held it up for her to see. She saw lots of numbers in columns, but didn't see them as bank balances because she wasn't interested in his money. He looked at her like a kindly grandfather. His voice was soft.

"You need anything, dress, shoes, you name it. I can take you downtown right now and get it. Nice-looking girl like you needing things, oughta have 'em, can have 'em."

She let his offer stay where it was. No, she didn't need anything, she told him. She didn't tell him she knew what girls paid for "free" money. She couldn't tell the old man what she thought of him; since babyhood, she had been taught to respect the old. Now respect translated into tolerating his talk and concealing a touch of amusement.

The old man used his powers again: "You been wondering about your boyfriend."

She had been wondering why she hadn't seen him much lately.

"Tall fellow, built likes a weight lifter. "He was so sure. Maybe he had seen them together, Juanita thought.

"He's not the one for you. He's for somebody else, but I can get him for you if you want him," the old man offered.

He told her that her boyfriend had two other girlfriends, one a little lighter, one a little darker than she. To get him, she had to write something on a slip of paper and put it under her telephone and get some of his hair-- or was it his fingernail?—and bury it near her back doorstep.

She didn't want anybody bad enough to go calling on the devil—that's what she believed working roots was. When she needed help, she called on the Lord, even in her dreams. The week before, she had dreamed about a mysterious man, old, dark. She had no idea who he was. When he got on an elevator with her, it lost control, rushing them toward the ground. She cried out, "Oh Lord, help me! Then the elevator slowed and floated like a cloud and she woke up.

The old man looked serious as he shook his head. "I can get him, but he's not for you."

She said nothing.

"What you need is somebody you know and trust, somebody older than you." Mr. Barnes' voice was low, confidential. He slowed the car a little and gave her a look like a doctor being frank with a patient. "Cause you needs some 'tention bad. Somebody can give you some good loving and keep it just 'tween you and him 'cause if you don't get some get some 'tention soon, you gone go crazy. Like that Thompson woman. When I was working at her house—remember it like it was yesterday—I was up there on the ladder in her kitchen—told her she needed some 'tention real bad. She didn't listen and she was in the crazy house two weeks later."

Juanita didn't know Mrs. Thompson, but she knew Mr. Thompson and his two teenaged sons and had heard about his wife being in the crazy house. But then the old man could tell her anything after the fact, she thought.

Minutes later, at the stop light, down the hill, past the overhead bridge, a few blocks from her school, the old man's arm was around her slim shoulders. The brush of his face against hers felt light, like a cobweb. Lips, rubbery, damp, slid along her cheek. Instantly, she jerked away. Her books were sliding off her lap. Her hand stopped them in time.

The old man's face clenched into dark gray ugliness. The blue eyes squeezed and deepened. Thunder gathered in his voice:

"I'm gonna make you rue the day you was ever born!"

Her voice came back, low, careful, but her look was straight at him. The look said, "I know what you are." But she said, "I don't believe in getting involved with anybody for money or what they can do for me. I would have to at least care about somebody and they would have to care about me."

The light was green. The car moved again. They were close to the school in a neighborhood of big brick houses with perfect lawns. "You right," he said after a while. He sounded almost repentant and looked better. "That's the way it should be."

Then he said, "You don't trust me, but I'm gonna bless you anyway."

Stopped in front of the school gym, where she had told him to let her out, he had another vision: "I see you got a hurdle coming, coming up soon, but you gon' get over it." There was approval in his eyes. "You got what it takes to make it."

She straightened her books, cradling them in her arms, and thanked him for the ride. He watched her get out of the car. She headed down the walkway and felt good to be out of the car. The big new red brick gym standing in the clearing across the street from the science building looked good, and the soft clean sunlight was good. She walked lightly toward the gym.

The old man's arm was along the back of the black vinyl seat. He leaned toward the passenger side, looking out the partly open window smiling as if he possessed a secret. She heard him say, "You'll be all right. Just keep thinking the way you thinking girl, and you gon' make it."

Joyce Compton Brown

The Dealer

Howard's palsied hands
jitterbug across yellowed plats
as he speaks of deeds,
ancient borders, deals he's
made for family lands.

His rusted-out Ford pickup,
groaning its half a million miles,
bucks up the gully-washed
red road of Pearlie's old place
throwing papers and caps,
cups and plastic junk
off the dashboard.

He'll trade this place
for our family field,
he says, wash-worn
overalls hanging
on his lanky bones
as he lights up,
coughs, takes a draw.

He'd scrambled up to grown
in one of those little hollows
left vacant by prosperous
farmers on the valley floor.
Now he collects trailer lots
flatland farms and old home
places, shuffles them all

like fifty-two pickup,
one more deal before
the last cough, the last
shaky hold before the fold.

Michael Gaspeny

Inaugural

In the park, I sniffed a late-blooming gardenia,
Mom's favorite flower, and talked to her,
gone twenty-nine years this January noon.

I hoped she heard kids squealing
on swings. She prized hijinks, rare
in her Depression girlhood of crop-stubble
and pickled tumbleweed. She chafed at ostentation,
made sure vacations included presidential shrines—
the Truman Library, Hyde Park, Garfield's Farm.

A buzzing drone blitzed the day—whirling chariot
manipulated by a gloating Goliath in a red ballcap
and camouflage jacket decorated by pawnshop medals.
The racket drowned the kids, my words to Mom.
I wanted to knock the drone down or tackle the Beast,
but he was off, working his joystick.

In the car, Springsteen lisped. At home, sounds dimmed.
I plunged below the squall, woke with my old ears,
but pressure wedged my skull like a hat I couldn't claw off.
How it would sicken Mom, every morning squeezing down.

Peter Venable

On My 71st

I bob on the S-shaped metal chair
in my screened-in back porch shrine.
Sip peach apricot black tea,
inhale rose hip, orange peel, peach
aromas as bee's honey soaks
my taste buds into euphoria.

A Tufted Titmouse squabbles at a Wren
drinking from a stainless-steel bowl.
They eye each other then
suddenly streak toward trees
as a large ebony shape lands
by the bowl, beak clamping on

a hamburger bun absurdly white
against purple-sheened feathers.
It scans 360, drops it in the water,
pecks over and over
until saturated, plops
the mushy bun on the deck

and savors morsel by morsel
like bread dipped in a chalice.
Preening, stretching wings, the Corvus
lifts toward the canopy and vanishes.
I raise my teacup in toast,
sip honey at the bottom of the cup

Colleen Lanier

Looking Up

Head down, I rushed down the sidewalk to my car, juggling my purse, keys, umbrella, and a bag of Home Depot leftovers I needed to return. I was running through the list of things I hoped to accomplish before my 6 pm meeting when a sound caught my attention, bringing me to a halt.

A soft thumping noise, faint but discernible, seemed to be close.

I couldn't place it. The sound didn't belong. I turned back toward my front door, and scanned the roof, the trees, and the fence line. The rustling, a soft rhythmic beating, continued. *Where is it coming from?*

I held perfectly still. It continued, the tempo of the thumping accelerating, then pausing ever so briefly.

Thump, thump, thump.

I walked back to my door, and there was movement in my peripheral vision as I passed the lamp post. Focusing on the light fixture, I found the source of the sound.

Behind the glass of the eight-sided lamp, a small cardinal, frantic, beat her wings against the walls. She jumped from bulb to bulb, flapping her wings and circling the confines of the hexagon.

I approached slowly, making what I hoped would be soothing bird noises, shushing her.

"Shhh, shh, shh, shh. Don't be afraid. I won't hurt you. Shh, shh, shh. How did you get in there, bird?"

My voice did nothing to calm her, and she circled even faster, flapping uncontrollably, right side up, then upside down, a blind panic.

"Okay, bird. Can I call you Ladybird? Let me see what I can do here."

I looked up, trying to formulate a plan. The black iron post was at least six feet high, and the light fixture sat atop it, balanced on four iron arms that supported the base of the lamp. Between the metal arms and the bottom edge of the glass, there was about an inch-and-a half of space. On top of the glass there was a black metal cap with an integral finial. A solid piece of metal with no opening. The bird had to have squeezed in from the bottom, forcing its way into the fixture. The four metal arms were screwed into the base of the fixture, and I thought I could remove the screws and lift the glass to release her

"Okay, Ladybird, I'm going inside to get a screwdriver and a ladder. Don't worry- I'll be back." I dropped my things inside the doorway, and grabbed a Philips head screwdriver and my step stool. I returned to the lamp post, causing an immediate escalation in her flapping.

"Shhh. It will be okay- I am going to get you out. Calm down, calm down. It will be okay."

I placed my stepstool on the damp earth, and, with my first step, it sunk and tilted, throwing me to the ground.

"Dammit!" I brushed myself off and tried again, putting a hand on the post to steady myself as I climbed. I loosened the first screw, and it fell into the Hosta below. "Dammit!" She hopped to the other side of the hexagon, as far away from me as possible.

"Sorry, Ladybird. It's okay. I will figure this out. We're both having a bad day, huh?"

I removed all four screws and tried to lift the glass off the post. The bird retreated up into the cap, momentarily quiet. Nothing happened. It didn't budge. I examined the fixture again, and noticed six tiny screws that held the cap in place. Plan B.

I continued to talk to the bird as I worked, releasing one screw at a time, carefully putting them in my pocket, making shushing sounds as I worked. She stayed opposite me as I circled, but seemed to be calmer.

"Almost there, Ladybird. This is going to work, and you can be on your way. Do you have babies somewhere? Waiting for you? Did you chase something into this lamp? You know that you can get out the same way you got in, right? All you had to do was hop out the bottom. Too bad you don't understand me." I missed my pocket, and screw #4 ended up in the Hosta.

"Dammit! It can't be easy, right? Not for people, not for birds." For a fleeting second, she tilted her head to the side. Listening. Empathizing. "You understand, right? It's always something."

The 6th and final screw fell into my hand, and I jiggled the cap to loosen it. She immediately jumped down to the bottom of the glass cage, seeking shelter under the arm of a candelabra bulb. Slowly, gently, I rocked the cap back and forth, and it reluctantly gave way in my hands. I lifted it off, and Ladybird was free.

She hopped onto the arm of the bulb she had been hiding under, shook out her feathers, and settled in, comfortable.

"You're free!"

She perched, content.

"I have errands to run, Ladybird. Shoo! Get going so I can put this lamp back together, ok? You're free!"

She didn't move. I shook the post slightly, and she jumped down to her hiding spot. She apparently didn't know she was free. *She wouldn't look up.*

"Look up! You can go! There is wide open sky right above your head!" I took a few steps down the sidewalk, hoping she would leave when I stepped away.

She didn't. I walked back towards her, using my arms to pantomime upward motion. My approach caused her to start circling the bottom of the fixture, wings once again thumping the glass. *She wouldn't look up.*

I rapped the bottom of the glass, trying to force her upwards and out. "Look up, Ladybird! Time to go!" I placed both my hands on the fixture, cradling the base to compel her ascent.

Finally, she hopped on top of a bulb, and looked up. She flapped her wings, and took flight. I put the lamp back together, took the stepstool and screwdriver into the house and gathered my things. I lingered on the sidewalk, enjoying the shade of the trees and the smell of the flowers.

Colleen Lanier **43**

I waited, thinking she would come back, or settle on a tree nearby to watch me. I half expected a *thank you for setting me free*. Apparently, she never looked back.

JoAnn Hoffman

A Boy, A Girl, An Orange

How young they were that day, *how young!*
how much in love with the wonder of love.

An orange sun drenched the hill they hiked,
made an apricot lake beneath the tree

where they floated the dazzling white picnic cloth
and lay out a most modest picnic indeed:

one ripe, brilliant orange between them.

She plunged a thumbnail deep into the rind
exploding a shower of yellow-red scent

that wrapped them around and hung in the heat
while peel fell like petals to cushion their feet.

He pried segments apart — a soft *chih-chih* sound,
made rings for her fingers with threads of white pith.

They fed one another criss-crossing their hands,
sticky-sweet juice trailing down their brown arms

one bold, brilliant orange between them.

She lay back on a jumble of peel, pulp and seeds
while he kissed the pale drops catching light on her chin,

the sharp tang of acid well hidden beneath
the glow of perfection in orange afternoons.

Gerard Berry

Refugees

#1

Crossing the border
      from Macedonia into Serbia,
  a wrinkled line
        of
           thirteen adults and children,
   heads downcast,
          pick   their way
        through   a frozen
                field.

     A girl
bundled in a scruffy pink and brown blanket
  carries plastic bags in her little arms.
    Hatless,
     she is first
    to spy the great
  transmission tower in front of them:
    Its peaked head,
   softly humming wires,
  curled coils and stout frame
hovers above low vaporous clouds.

    "Daddy,"
    she cries.
  "Daddy... look!
   Look up!
  See the angel?"

2

Day breaks on the city of bank towers.
Drivers disgorge from parking garages,
collars raised and frames bent into the wind.
They walk past the dark, skull-capped man
who sits bundled in a newspaper kiosk
waiting to make his first sale.

She too, hurries
in a top-buttoned, gray wool coat
and blowing garnet tail of scarf.
A mousy, sometime customer,
she glances in, her heart pounding.
His torched, defeated face softens as she nears.
Others look in, avert, and pass in droves.
They both jump when a truck backfires,
and share a relieved nod and smile.
The smell of stale sweat encloses her;
the stacks of papers enwall them.

To shore herself up, she sings
with silent lips, *"Give me your
tired, your poor,
your huddled masses yearning
to breathe free."*

She has owned her fear of strangers,
but fears his fears are greater,
this alien pitching to an alien crowd.
She loves the trust in this other's eyes,
and trusts the love in her own.

"I'll take five," she says, like a colossus,
golden-gloved hand raised like a lamp.
He takes her money and bows delicately,

mirroring gratitude.

Send me these.

1

Refugees
#3

Today the cruise ship docks at Piraeus.
You follow the guide to vans which
take you past the swarming refugee tents to Athens,
where you check your bags at the Hilton Hera.
This afternoon you see the Acropolis,
roam the Agora, buy gifts, then return to freshen up.

Tonight you dine by Homer's wine-dark sea.
Your husband commends your elegant choice of gown.
You finger an absence of one of your rings,
missing since you met the Syrian girl
in the line outside the relief center.

What's the matter now, he asks.
You haven't touched your crème brulee.
He sends it back to be reheated
and asks the sommelier for a desert wine.
Nothing, you say. Nothing's wrong at all.

Mary Hennessy

Life Line

The pier at Kure Beach, memoried
cathedral, slat-ribbed
shanty of silk and fish-line ,
shelters the man held
up and together by red suspenders.
The metal lunch pail at his side
empty. His wife quiet.

    Come on baby, he says, *come on.*
The anchor on the line he casts—flies past seeing
then sinks and holds firm to the sea floor.
The live bait on the "fighting line" cartoonish,
restive—as mackerel swim in to see what's up

    Come on baby.
Silver fish berserk in the motions of a fast getaway
skip like stones across the surface.
Sand sharks under the pier twist
in the furious churn beneath
the scarred metal table where fish,
caught are ritually cleaned.
The drain, round as a stovepipe, drops
the chum into the saltwater—
makes everything look rosy.

The fisherman's wife wears the same hat
she wears to church.
The best bait for mackerel are the shiny
ones, she says,

as she reaches up to touch
a pink fabric rose to be sure it's still there.
You know the hook will break
his heart.

Donna Love Wallace

EACH STEP

Ankles buckled
in snake skin heels—
still working on the walk.

Backless sundress,
fluttering ruffles flushing
a heavy hip swing.

Swaying a new
dress daily,
this fluidity

I envy. Each step,
his blush of silk
becomes him.

Esther Whitman Johnson

UNDER THE SOUTHERN CROSS

"I like your hat," my neighbor calls from his car

"Thanks, it's from Africa," I say, not bothering with specifics. African geography's not a strong suit around here. But this hat of pink, green, and yellow is not just *from Africa*; it's *from Monique*—a parting gift from the family who took me into their home, loved me like a sister, like an auntie, and cried when I left. The ten days I spent with them were among the toughest in my life, and their faces are imprinted forever in my memory.

It began with a man who wouldn't go by the book, who refused to follow procedure, who lived and worked in Antananarivo, the capital of Madagascar, far removed from our remote village. I never knew the man, the in-country Director of Habitat for Humanity, but he made a unilateral decision that had a lasting impact on me and our team. The volunteers were originally scheduled to sleep in a completed Habitat house on the floor in sleeping bags. We would use the latrine and solar shower there when we returned at night after working on three new houses all day. *That's* what we signed on for.

But the Director altered the plan *after* our arrival in Africa—definitely against protocol—and assigned us all to local families who were paid five dollars a day to house us. Good money in Africa. Competition to host us was fierce, and being selected was a matter of honor more than money. The Director, who sat in his office hours away from our village, put into place an untried plan that had consequences he could not have imagined. Some volunteers rebelled and refused to budge from the headquarters house, while others stayed one night with villagers and returned, claiming to be too much trouble for the hosts; then the unfortunate host families were hurt, wondering what they'd done wrong. Altogether a sensitive, sticky predicament.

One steadfast volunteer stayed with her family even after picking up a bad case of lice from the little girl with whom she shared a single bed. The only African-American on the team, the volunteer felt she owed it to the family to be a role model and live as they did. Team members argued long and hard over the situation the first few days: were we *forced* to live in African homes or *privileged* to live in them? I kept my mouth shut, laid low, and stayed with my family, but not because I'd made a moral decision to take the high road; I was simply one lucky woman, in far better circumstances than most of the others.

The Director would not budge on the issue. "Westerners," he said, "come to help, and they mean well, but they haven't a clue. To know the real Africa, you must live with the people."

On that point, he was right.

"*Voulez-vous une douche chaude?*" Monique asked me, as we walked into her house at ten o'clock the first night. Covered with dirt from the build, I stank, embarrassed to stand next to her in her clean clothes—Western clothes worn to work as secretary to the village mayor. *A shower,* I thought, *a lovely tile shower, hot water running down my back.*

"*Oui, merci beaucoup,*" I said.

Monique spoke French, one of an entire generation educated in public schools run by France before independence. Good thing, because I knew not a word of Malagasy. That's not to say I actually *spoke* French, but I *understood* most of what she said, which was way more than the non-French speakers who lived with the other villagers. It was pure luck that I had looked over some French before I went and actually took a French dictionary—all the

Habitat information had said that the only language was Malagasy.

As for the shower, it was anything but the tiled luxury of my vision. Since the neighborhood well had closed at seven p.m., Monique rounded up eight-year-old Rina and sent her to the river with two buckets for water while she fired up the wood stove to heat it.

"Oh, no, don't send Rina out in the dark for me," I protested. But my decades-old French failed, and I stood by helplessly as the little girl left, flashing me the toothy smile I would come to love.

Twenty minutes later, carrying only my towel, I followed Monique out back to the communal shower house, separated from the communal latrine by a rickety wooden partition. A man was peeing on the other side, but I didn't want to know who. Monique left me with the two buckets, patted my back, and smiled. *"Bien, très bien."*

"Oui, merci."

I figured I'd wash out my work clothes as I'd done at night on other Habitat builds, but the water wouldn't stretch that far. So, keeping my underwear on, I threw my work clothes outside, figuring no matter how dirty the ground was, it was better than putting anything down inside the smelly shack. Holding my nose against the stench of the latrine, I hoisted a bucket with one hand and poured, trying to wash hair, body, and underwear with two small pails of fast-cooling water. Neither my hair nor my underwear got rinsed, and both dried stiff and scratchy.

Back inside, Monique led me up the ladder to her bed in the large loft; she and the four children would crowd into the tiny room downstairs, sleeping on the floor. She pointed out the new print curtains and cover for the straw mattress she'd just finished for me. Two posters of scantily-clad women decorated the wall—one a blond, buxom Westerner, the other a sultry Asian—both advertising life insurance. Their pouty lips and protruding bottoms were the last things I saw before I closed my eyes at night, awake for hours, straw poking my back, dust kicking off my allergies.

I will not take another shower, I decided, as I tossed and turned that first night. *I will not let the eight-year-old trek to the river every night. I will not let Monique spend her limited free time waiting on me.* And I stuck to it. For ten days, I washed at night in the loft with Wet Ones. For ten days, I wrapped my filthy hair inside a bandana. For ten days, I wore the same three

t-shirts and two pairs of jeans. In my nightmares—and there were many—my clothes stood on their own, saluted, and marched around the loft like soldiers on parade.

I was starting to know Africa. The Director would have been pleased.

Each morning I woke to the smell of coffee and the whispers of the children below. I rose quickly to pee in the green plastic bucket I'd bought to avoid going out to the neighborhood latrine in the middle of the night. Like a tight rope walker, I balanced over the bucket, aiming carefully, so nothing would miss and drip between the floor planks. How mortifying it would be to pee on my family below! Quiet as I tried to be, I knew they could hear me downstairs. There is no privacy in an African house.

No sooner than I'd finished my business, the kids would pop up the ladder, bringing my breakfast tray—coffee, bread, jam, eggs, fruit, some kind of meat. What kind of meat I didn't know, didn't ask, and didn't eat.

Six-year-old Tonjana sat on my lap like a little emperor, playing with my face, my fingers, my shirt, ordering the older kids to sit on the floor.

"Let's count," said one child.

"Let's braid your hair," said another.

"Let's sing."

"Let's dance."

"Let's sing and dance."

Same thing every day, first thing in the morning, last thing at night. The kids spoke neither English nor French, but we understood each other. We giggled, tickled, turned on the battery radio, and danced like crazy people. And hugged. Always hugs—four hugs from the kids in the loft and one from Monique on my way out the door headed to the building site.

Breakfast was always too much, so I offered part of it to the kids, who refused it every time. Three days into my stay, I realized that my breakfast was the only breakfast Monique fixed. What I didn't eat became the morning meal for five people, who waited to see what I left. From that day on, I ate only an egg and a piece of fruit at Monique's. My lunch and dinner were provided by Habitat—huge meals, with leftovers I stuffed into bags to bring home to the kids. Against the rules, but I did it anyway.

On Sunday I walked through the village, searching for the Lutheran Church I'd seen one day from the work van. I heard the drone of the familiar liturgy wafting down the street long before I arrived. Why I found it comforting, I don't know, because I'm not particularly religious. The words of the liturgy were Malagasy, but the cadence was Lutheran, and I knew it well. I loitered at the door, content to stay outside, too timid to wade into the sea of black bodies, certain I did not belong.

Suddenly a tiny, sweaty hand slid into mine—little Tonjana, sent by Monique to make sure I didn't get lost. Tonjana, always in charge, wouldn't let me stand back, but pulled me into the church all the way to the front.

No, not here, I don't belong here. I wanted to run, but I was stuck with my little African 'brother', who would not let go of my hand.

Every pew was full, but Tonjana found a place for me on the floor with the kids. A few minutes later a woman tapped my shoulder, pointed to a place beside her, and the whole row of women—very large women—squeezed together to put me where they insisted I belonged, no matter how much I shook my head. One woman brushed dust from my pants, pulled me to her, and thrust the hymnal into my hand. I did as I was instructed—sat, stood, knelt, sang, and stayed all the way through *Lord, now let thy servant depart in peace.*

From the altar, a statue of white Jesus looked down upon the congregation, his blue eyes kind. And no one but me seemed to find him out of place.

On the last day of the build, our team hung out on the porch of the Habitat headquarters house, waiting for dinner. Every day the same ritual: the kids came running to play, chat, draw, dance, and sing with us. We built houses all day and interacted with the villagers in the evening, until we fell into bed, utterly exhausted. Unlike other builds, where volunteers said goodbye to the locals, went back to a hotel, cleaned up, had a glass of wine, and ate relaxed meals by themselves, the Africa build put us "on" all day and all night. We were tired and it showed; by the last night we had almost lost the energy to laugh.

The twelve-year-old girl who followed me everywhere grabbed my hand and dragged me into the street. Some kid brought out a boom box, and the music blasted through the square. The lyrics were intoxicating, and soon we were all in the street, singing and dancing, screaming, and stinking. They probably understood not a word, but the Malagasy children belted out the song in English, singing along with the tape and us:

> *We are the world, we are the children*
>
> *We are the ones who make a brighter day . . .*
>
> *It's true we'll make a better day*

Just you and me . . .
Let's realize a change can only come
When we stand together as one . . .
We are the world . . .

(Michael Jackson)

Even if the kids didn't understand the words, they understood the sentiment. And as we linked arms and swayed in the dusk in that muddy street in Africa, perhaps I understood the words for the first time.

Late that night Monique and I sat on her stoop under a canopy of stars—The Southern Cross lighting up the night sky—chatting, saying everything but *goodbye*. Reaching out, she pressed the hat of many colors into my hand and said, "A souvenir to remember us, to remember Africa."

As if I could forget.

"*Les étoiles sont différentes ici,*" I said, looking to the heavens to avoid looking at her. The sky was so unlike that in the Northern Hemisphere that I was thrown off balance every time I looked at the stars.

"*Oui,*" said Monique. "*Tout c'est différent ici.*"

Yes, everything was different. I was in Africa.

Now, when I wear my pink, green, and yellow hat I remember Africa. But I can no more explain it to my neighbors than anyone could have explained it to me.

Lucas Hargis

Grandmama's Ghost Stories

My grandmama clad in silver & turquoise
jewelry collected while working at truckstops
homeward backtracking that Trail of Tears
from Oklahoma, told me stories
On North Carolina pond banks fishing for bream
Once, young as you, sick as a dog
with a fit of high fever
my dead aunt came to me clear as day
Red & white planets bobbed at the far ends
of invisible lines stretched like spiderwebs
from our cane poles to the still water
skimmed by lucky dragonflies
& my favorite aunt swabbed my little girl forehead
soft as a dove's coo
with the back of her ghost hand whispering
It'll be alright, baby. It'll be alright
Patiently waiting, sweating, laughing until
bammm a fish took that juicy worm
My fever instantly broke
& I was all better
And a yank, not too hard though
hopefully sinking the brass hook
into supper's mouth
One morning on my way to school
swishing through a path worn to clay
in that tall grass, a white dog appeared
out of nowhere
Sometimes a silly Eastern Box Turtle

accidentally snagged the hook under
the edge of its shell as it swam past
I stopped. Unafraid of that strange dog
I'd never seen before so much as curious
why it blocked my way
easing closer to me when I stepped towards it
backing up when I did
So we'd just set the turtle free
replace that pale, bloated worm with a fresh one
& cast out again
An ugly snake fatter than a pine trunk
slithered out beyond that shimmering dog
Biggest, plumpest, scariest snake
ever seen in them parts
Appalachian sun pinked my freckled skin
Grandmama's deepened ruddier & ruddier
That mysterious white dog calmly held me
with its steady gaze while that hungry snake
stretched & slithered & stretched forever
across the very spot I would've been standing
had that dog not come
When Grandmama prayed the clouds in
& coolness kissed us, both our bobbers
dunked at once
That snake tapered down to the tip of its tail
finally slipping out of sight in them weeds
Two fish in our bucket, then four, up to seven
me pulling in the extra as Grandmama packed up
before the first raindrop splashed the windshield
the second we slammed
her old truck's doors closed
The dog vanished quick as it'd come
I went on to school because I wouldn't dare be late
Never saw that dog or snake ever again
We scaled our catch
cleaned & sliced them bream

into delicate fillets
There was this old verse or saying about
well, something along the lines of
flying to you on the wings of a white dove
to let you know I'm safe
Salted, peppered, fried in Crisco & a cast-iron skillet
Cole slaw & hushpuppies on the side
Better than any truckstop
Enough sweet tea sipped to give you the sugars
but might as well go happy
When your truck driving grandpapa died
before you were born
I rocked on the side porch to ease
my heart broken with the missing of him
So I drew a crayon picture of an angel
for her while she hummed
& washed the dishes
And a pair of doves landed
right in front of me
Didn't peck around the yard for worms
or bugs like usual. Both lingered there
tilting their heads & looking at me
And I knew it was J.B.
letting me know
he was in heaven
Oh my goodness. Let me hug your neck, baby
This is so pretty. Imagine that
Me with a grandson
who's gonna be a famous artist
You just wait & see if I aint right about that
I wear truckstop jewelry nowadays
dotted with turquoise & silver speckles of paint
that wipe right off
You dry them tears now. I'm gonna visit
Haven't gone pond fishing or even touched
a cane pole in too long a time

But I can season cast iron
& walk well-worn trails
swish new ones through them weeds
when I'm lonely
feeling doves coo feathery soft
I'm here, I love you, you're safe
It'll be alright, baby
It'll be alright

Sam Barbee

Mirror Image
- Mabry Mill, Blue Ridge Parkway, 1996

Photo by the lake:
    my wife holds two bags of stone-ground flour;
    our young son stands, arms crossed, happy,
        smiling on command;
    and younger daughter stands, arms crossed, unhappy,
        because *lots of things* —
    ready to inventory them, like scuffle of fallen leaves
        across the water.

Beside the mill,
    two seventy-something travelers at a split-rail fence;
        hands grip top-rail,
    risk hickory splinters. Do they notice our family
        dressed for travel . . .
    what might they think of us: did we map our journey
        here . . .
    highlight a clear route home? This opaque day

hardened clouds cover us all.
    The couple's image floats center-lake, wavering
        while pristine, encircled
    by cast-leaves' constellations; dammed-in
        by the mill's stone foundation
    and grassy banks. We all pause, align ourselves
        like the water wheel;
    each hewn stone burnished, hand-laid to hem us
        inside this neutral plain.

Reflections ripple, benign
       wrinkles – our separate flocks focusing south,
            people to weather
    do's and don'ts, rights and less-rights, lost, found,
            and lost.
    As the older couple pivots, I invite my daughter to smile,
            and persuade
    myself to exhale, certain all saints, departed or gathered,
            wish us well.

Camilla Wilcox

Standing in Line at Food Lion

With the sweet gentleness of old age,
He clutches the heavy, dirty pot against his chest,
Where, long ago, he held his newborns
Cradled in arms brown and strong from sun and plow.
He smiles now as he smiled then.
Dry, crusty soil coats his highbibs and dusts the floor around him
When he reaches into the frayed chest pocket for a handful of coins.

A June Pink, by chance the last plant left on the grocer's shelf,
But still, his choice
In case the time left is too short to wait for summer's end.
He remembers then Better Boy and Beef Steak and Golden Queen
Lined up, shoulder to shoulder, on dish towels
In the hot, hot, August kitchen,
Where steam erupted from simmering pots of water
And misted his glasses.
He remembers then shining jars of summer bounty lined up,
Three-deep, on cellar shelves.

From acres of rows and cages,
Rough split wooden stakes and ripped muslin ties,
Hotbeds in winter, transplants in spring,
Tractors, wheelbarrows, buckets, boxes, baskets,
Battered beds of ancient pick-up trucks,
And bags, endless bags, of tomatoes and coins,
It has come to this:
One wilted, twisted plant
One cracked plastic pot,
One green-stained bamboo stake,

Clip-on ties, and
A cloud of whiteflies fleeing his touch,
Exact change at Food Lion.

Most days, his reach extends
Not far from the folding chair in the carport,
Where he passes fair-weather hours
Near the ghost of the dooryard garden—
        A sunken square of clay and clods
        Draped in Bermuda grass and sedge.

From his chair, he can see the black iron post
That still holds the fading silver sign, handpainted:
        Tomatoes for Sale
        Fifty Cents a Pound
And the banged-together table,
Where each summer morning he arrayed
Rainbow arcs of crimson and gold, scarlet and pink;
Balanced his old scales; and
Placed a new pack of brown paper sacks in a slot
Next to the rusty, old tackle box marked
Leave Money Here.

Beside his chair, this year,
This June Pink will be enough
For watering and fertilizing,
For staking and tying,
For checking for insects,
For clipping suckers and yellowing leaves,
For sniffing tomato perfume on yellow-stained fingertips,
For counting new buds,
For waiting for petals to form and then fall
And the first fruit to emerge,
Like a baby's head crowning at birth.

Philip Lawton

After the Leaves Have Fallen

Almost home. First time in months. The overnight gatehouse attendant is a big-boned woman I've never met. I give her my name, pull ahead when the lift arm rises, drive slowly, watch for deer, fox, opossum.

The house stands dark. I push my wife over to her half of the bed, stretch my back muscles, try to find a comfortable position. I don't sleep well, even here, haven't, now, for years, just slumber, drifting in and out of semi-consciousness, but for once I have no commitments, and at daybreak I finally drop into oblivion. It's noon by the time I have coffee, catch up with my wife, head down to my study on the terrace level.

The air is dank.

I work for an investment management firm in southern California. My wife, set in her ways, prefers to stay in Virginia. It works for us. She is more independent than she used to be, a twenty-first century California widow, and we communicate better than we did, with frequent emails, daily telephone conversations, weekly Skype sessions. But, living on the first floor of the big house, she has no occasion to go downstairs. In this year's southern summertime, she did not remember to check the dehumidifiers, nor, in my absence, did I think to remind her.

"It's not the heat," my father once said, "it's the stupidity." The mustiness I smell now is black mold.

My first thought goes to my books. On a cursory inspection there's no visible fungus. Good. I follow my nose to the other rooms. The sailfish my son caught off Key West when he was nine—a burdensome prize that has followed us from house to house over the years; we call it Bill Fish—has mold in its mouth, frozen open, gasping for oxygen. Inky smudges stain the wall near the floor in the unused bedroom, over the tub in the bathroom, by the water heater in the utility room. But the worst of it turns up in a jumbled back room that the previous owners reserved for exercise machines and we use to store the flotsam of our life: baby gates, board games, baseball gloves.

I pick up one of my father's racing skates. The thin leather of the low black boot is cracked, the 15-inch blade rusty, one of the eyelets broken. There is mold on the toe. I stand there in the damp unfinished room, skate in hand, and remember a wintry Saturday morning in Connecticut.

I stood in my cramped bedroom, a room made oddly smaller by the Swedish red of its walls, and I dressed for the weather, long johns, blue jeans, red flannel shirt, Irish fisherman's sweater, red knit cap, navy woolen gloves. I did not take my hockey skates, scuffed and gouged from scrappy pick-up games on a farm pond in Bloomfield. This day cried out for poetry, called for the speed skates I'd found in the attic, brought back to life with neatsfoot oil, honed by hand on the workbench in the basement. I slipped out of the house, started my mother's grey Cutlass, drove down Asylum Avenue toward Hartford, the heater warming my legs but the window open for the frosty morning air. Just past my girlfriend's parents' brick house, still shuttered at that hour, I turned into the park Wallace Stevens loved, pulled up to the pond house, grabbed the skates, laced them up on a wooden bench.

A thin man was the only other skater; we waved but did not speak. The snow was bright, the air cold, the ice glassy, deep, with a smooth patina, marred only by a few scratches here and there from the thin man's figure skates. I propelled myself through a fast circuit, up the west side of the bigger pond, under the arch of the stone bridge, around the lily pond, and back, then settled into a steadier, more deliberate pace, knees bent, shoulders forward, arms swinging. My mouth dried, nostrils froze, but my torso stayed warm. I stopped to catch my breath, wished I'd worn sunglasses, noticed I was sweating. I strode on my blades to the pond house for a cup of hot chocolate, the thin kind they made with cocoa powder and water, no marshmallow or whipped cream, really nothing more than an excuse to sit indoors for a few minutes at the risk of burning my mouth. Then I went back to the ice. My legs were strong, lungs clear, movements sure and easy. I thought I could skate like that forever, glide through life, write the next great American novel, tour the country, win the Pulitzer, write the screenplay for a major motion picture. But in my mind I heard my mother's gentle laughter and soft voice: "Delusions of grandeur, dear."

I drop the skate, climb the stairs, find my wife in the sunroom, tell her about the mold. She calls a remediation service. They seal the terrace level with plastic sheeting, bring in a commercial HEPA vacuum, wipe down the books, one by one, spray biocides on all the hard surfaces, tear up the rugs, install an industrial dehumidifier. Wearing garden gloves and respiratory masks, my son and I work our way through the storage room, bag toy cars, canteens, cassettes, tote the bags to the street for disposal. He wants to rescue loose photographs; I am more inclined to discard the whole box. He holds up the ice skates. "What's the story with these?" I tell him to throw them away.

Packing for California at the end of the week, I take the worn paperback edition of Stevens's collected poems from my bookcase. In college I read his poetry aloud, puzzled over it, finally just reveled in the language, the eloquent English and apposite French. I was fascinated by the way he managed his two worlds, compartmentalized them, composing poems on the two-mile walk up Asylum Avenue to his office at the Hartford, then turning his mind to logic and law. When I first went to work at Aetna, and later at the Travelers, I found proof in his life that a man could support a family and still create works of art. Both of us went to meetings, wrote memos, entertained clients in the executive dining room. I wondered if, like me, he scanned the sports pages in order to fake his way through the lunchtime conversation, pass for the guy next door. Had our careers overlapped, we might have found each other at the Hartford Club or the Canoe Club, might have raised a glass, then another, talked about our houses, wives, children, debated the place of imagery in philosophy and poetry.

I tried to put a narrative on paper, bargained with myself, tried again, then postponed the effort—it wasn't a good time, it was never a good time, my job was too demanding, my family—and finally let it go. The children grew up, graduated, left home, came back, left again. It made no difference. Life came down to work.

My son sees me off at the airport. Seated on the westbound flight, I open the book to one of the poems Stevens set in the park. The leaves have fallen, the greenhouse needs paint, the great pond is muddy, its lilies wasted. It is hard, the poet confesses, to find the right word to describe "this blank cold, this sadness without cause." But he has to imagine the absence of imagination. I do not. And suddenly I see how I sabotaged myself, how my compromises conspired to wash away the wonder. Nobody stopped me from writing stories, my parents, wife, children are not to blame, it's all my doing, the lassitude, laziness, *lacheté* are mine. The mold is mine.

I set the poetry aside and turn to a commentary on the capital markets. The flight attendant brings me a miniature bottle of whiskey and a plastic cup of ice.

Wyatt Bond

Photo

I keep a photo in my wallet
my brother's face slowly scratched away
rubbed nearly white
across the back of embossed credit-card numbers
and old, wrinkled dollars

his hair wild, and curly,
windblown and twisted
above blue eyes, barely bloodshot
from a warm morning
of Arizona dust

a fold in the photo
left there when I transferred
the memory of his face
from one piece of worn leather
to a dollar store wallet
and then to something more grown up

the fold lies across the nose I broke
when we were kids fighting over nothing
ending with him in a crumpled heap
on the floor, not even crying
just full of younger brother rage

his lips are curved upward in a smile
revealing teeth I can't even tell are fake
the real ones lost on some steep driveway

unfortunate casualties of a rollerblade accident
which began as a dare

the bottom corners of the photo
are dog eared and faded,
his black shirt grey in some spots
and gone altogether in others,
victims of my habit of taking him out time and again
just to sit and smile back at him

Diana Engel

Walnut Heart

My wide-grinning dad,
you held in your palm
midnight mica,
rocks gathered on beach walks,
confessing you couldn't spot sharks' teeth
or sunset-hued scallops in the sand.

Black like the heart of the green walnuts
that covered our West Tennessee front yard,
plummeting near the rope and board swing.
When you pushed me, I would fly up
and back down to earth--
my stomach bottoming out
as my legs pumped into tree-paned sky.

Beach vacations
you would sit in a lawn chair,
daddy feet in the surf,
read the paper as we rode waves into shore.
What did we know of death
until you died
and we became seagulls
winging through morning,
believing you would appear at water's edge
if only we would wait.

Now older than you,
I walk my dog through the woods,
stepping over knuckled roots,

treading the worn path
that circles Oak Hollow Lake.

In the call of geese crossing water,
I hear an ache,
remember pungent walnut husk
as scent of last night's rain rises
from the earth.

Michael Boccardo

Potboilers

She savored the classics most: *Peyton Place,*
Valley of the Dolls, Scruples. Dickens was snubbed.
Tolstoy a crutch for the family sofa.
To each life shelved inside her, my mother said
yes. Yes to Greek tycoons & cocktails swilled
above the Caribbean's rose-tinted cliffs. Here,
she was single, childless. Reckless. Pursued by lovers
down a Parisian boulevard, or boarding a jet bound
for exotic seas. She hid her grief this way:
raised a husband, sons, skipped the chapter that fit
her parent's eyes for coin. Brazen, she'd turn
a page, flee elsewhere—mistress, heiress,
Russian Contessa—her body a chandelier
of diamonds. But she always returned, breathless,
scented in scarves of lilac & gardenia.
Unlike now, her memory diminished, barely
a footnote, a coda. This lament of silk,
these fingers a jeweled echo. Into her epilogue
she wanders, but never arrives.

Allen Guest

The Smell of Heaven

In heaven it will always be
1964, probably May, or perhaps
early June. Heaven will be in the
backyard of our house in Toccoa, in
a little post-war neighborhood, homes
all neat and rectangular, with
modest red brick,
off-white trim, and dads who
arrive at 5:15 wearing
wing-tips and narrow ties, carrying
briefcases boxy as their houses.

In heaven my mother sits
at the picnic table
in our backyard
in the shade of the big water oak.
She wears
khaki Bermuda shorts, a yellow
sleeveless blouse, and
big sunglasses. She relaxes
with a cigarette, her reward for
hanging laundry on the clothesline.
She flicks ashes into
an empty coffee cup and listens for
baby brother's cry through
an open window.

She thinks about
Jackie Kennedy as she watches me,

four years old, running barefoot on
the smooth lawn my
father mowed yesterday.
I laugh, weave back and
forth between parallel rows
of white sheets that billow
in an easy breeze. They brush
cool and clean and damp
on my arms, legs, and
shirtless little-boy body. I fly
in a big white cloud
that smells like
Ivory Snow,
bleach, cut grass, and
cigarettes smoked by
Jackie Kennedy moms
in backyards
in 1964.

Anthony Howcroft

THE KING'S MEN VIGILANTES

The police advised everyone to avoid the woods, but that's like an invitation, isn't it?

I couldn't persuade the rest of our shift to join us, though. They were too scared, caught up in silly superstitions. Not many people want to venture into Whitare woods on a normal Saturday night, but especially not now, when there's a nutter about.

"Are we vigilantes?" Scott asks.

"Yep," Dex says.

"Officially, we're part of the Shelley Neighbourhood Watch Scheme," I say.

Scott switches the torch on and swings the beam around experimentally, but it's not dark enough for it yet.

"What shall we call ourselves?" Dex asks.

"The Panthers?" Scott says.

"Sounds like a Football team. What about the King's Men?" Dex counters.

I toss a stone into the bushes. "I'm not sure we want to be vigilantes."

The others look at me like I'm crazy.

"Vigilantes take the law in to their own hands. If vigilantes catch the weirdo they might beat the shit out of him, or string him high from that oak," I gesture.

"What's wrong with that?" Scott says.

"You're assuming it's a man?" Dex adds, with his thick local burr.

I laugh, "How many women would dress as a sadistic clown to scare people?"

Dex shakes his head in apparent disbelief at my stupidity.

"The King's Men," Scott says, defusing the situation. "I like that."

Nobody has mentioned a destination, but we're being pulled towards the Stone as if it were a magnet. The Stone sits on the hilltop, with a panoramic view for miles. As kids, Scott and I used to climb the Stone and sit there, gazing at the chequered fields that made up our world. These days, it's encircled by a small iron fence, and a warning sign that forbids touching, advising that the Council will prosecute any offenders. I'm not sure who let them take ownership of our Stone. Anyway, if I were a crazy killer-clown, the Stone is where I'd hang-out.

"Look at this bad boy," Scott says.

He points at a huge snail climbing a fence post. He flicks the torch on to illuminate the shell, and the snail's antennae withdraw as though the light were fire.

"What a whopper," says Dex, studying it carefully. "Wish I had some salt."

"That's for slugs," I say.

"A snail's only a slug with a shell," Dex says.

"That's like saying Jenny Widdup is a boy with tits," I tell him.

"I think you'll find there's a couple of other differences between boys and girls," Dex winks at Scott.

The snail's antennae slowly telescope back out, the right one moving faster than the left.

"We used to toss them into the sea," Scott says.

Dex has his face by the snail, inspecting it like a car engine.

Scott continues, "We'd see who could throw them furthest. They're the wrong shape for skimming."

"Let's go," I say, shoving Scott in the back, who's easy to shift, and slapping Dex to nudge him towards the steep slope leading to the crest. "Didn't know I was with two serial snail-killers."

Our breathing punctuates the air as we lean into the hill. I try to remember if antennae is the right word, of if snails possess eye stalks or tentacles. Perhaps there's a special snail-word. I could ask Dex, our self-appointed expert who freely doles out advice on all topics, but I'm not convinced science is his speciality.

"Did the salt water kill the snails?" Dex asks Scott.

"Well, none of them swam back to shore," Scott laughs.

"Did they melt?" Dex persists.

"I think they drowned."

The incline reduces, and we pause near the crest. The sun is low, and at this angle the Stone is hidden. The top of the hill is quartered, with the Stone in the centre. The left two quadrants are thick with scrub and trees, corralled behind barbed wire as though they might escape. That area is a labyrinth of animal trails, abandoned to kids, and teenagers holding illicit meetings. On the other side, the nearest quadrant has a scattering of gorse that gradually opens to a field sweeping down the hill towards Brough Road, a mile away. It's similar on the far side, except for a group of twenty loosely clustered trees standing beyond the crown, a respectful distance from the Stone. There's a thirty-yard gap clear of bushes between the two right hand quadrants, that slopes downhill with three natural steps which alter the gradient from severe, to steep, to gentle. That's where everyone goes sledging in winter.

"What's the plan if we find the clown?" Scott asks.

Dex nods in my direction, "He can run to the Neighbourhood Watch and fill in a form," he says. "While we kick the crap outta him. Or her."

"Perfect," Scott says.

"Should I bring you back some salt?" I say, sarcastically.

Scott puts a finger to his lips. Edging over the crest, we crouch. Scott takes the lead, and moves along the gorse, so we get a view of the whole area and stay hidden. Nobody is there, apart from the Stone. Not sure what I was expecting. A circus of cavorting clowns? Jenny Widdup with a pentacle daubed on her bare skin?

Scott gestures along one side of the dark hedge-line and points to Dex and I, indicating our route. I think his plan is for us to flush out any lurkers, while he waits in ambush. He's watched too many war films, with his ridiculous commando-signals, and not enough horror - never split up, that's the golden rule.

Dex sets off, stooped low, and Scott does the same in the opposite direction. I should have said something but nobody listens to me, so I follow Dex.

"How do they breathe?" I say, as I pull alongside him in a sandy dip.

"Who?" Dex whispers.

"Snails. Do they have lungs, or take oxygen through osmosis, like toads?"

"Does it matter?"

"They might not drown. They might be able to breathe under water."

Dex strains his neck to scan the horizon. I think for a moment he might have seen a clown, but I realise he's trying to locate Scott. An orange sunbeam hits the peak, and the Stone is spot lit, casting a shadow in our direction like a giant sundial. The light makes the Stone glow, as if the rock were translucent.

"King Eardwulf," Dex murmurs, referring to the legend.

"I wonder who put it there, and why?" I ask.

"It was the old woman. He should have run her through with his – "

"She was a witch, not some old woman," I correct him.

Dex laughs. "Same thing," then grins. "Let's have some fun with Scott. "

That sounds like a bad idea. I should say no, but experience tells me Dex will trample over my objections.

" Here's what we do," he says.

Scott sits hidden in the undergrowth, watching shadows twist across the hill. There's a solid wall of blackthorn to his right, hawthorn on the left, and a narrow path behind. He focuses on the scene in front, where the sun has formed a pool of orange light that flows gently towards the Stone. There was a jester in the old legend, he remembers, who threatened to roast the witch, claiming she was no more useful than a bag of sticks. Scott tries to recall what happened to the witch after she turned the King into rock, and what became of the jester, but the story has faded into his childhood. A bird, or possibly a rabbit, disturbs the leaves behind him.

Rolling up his jean leg, Scott unclips his knife, and feels the weight in his hand. It's a 1915 Imperial German S98/05 engineer's bayonet, a Duisberg. He passes a finger along the blade, where the original sawtooth has been ground off. Even toothless, it would be no laughing matter for any clown it encountered. To get this treasure, he'd traded a couple of WWII British pig stickers, and a modern parachute regiment issue that his brother had filched.

The late sun found the Stone. The subtle play of shadow on the wind-roughened surface gave the illusion of a crowned man. Scott slipped over a low strand of barbed wire and moved closer to the King Stone, the long bayonet clasped in his right hand.

A maniacal burst of laughter from beyond the copse made Scott swivel. As if the sun had been switched off, the Stone went black, plunging the hilltop into darkness. Something shifted in the scene, a flicker of movement from the Stone.

Two minutes earlier

It was a simple plan. One of us would creep behind the Stone, hidden by shadow and slope. The other would sneak below the brow of the hill, past the wild hares, and create a distraction on the right. When Scott emerged to investigate, the hider would rush Scott on his blindside and take him out with a rugby tackle, giving him the fright of his life. I wanted to be the distraction, but Dex pulled rank, or at least age.

"You're quicker than me," he said. "He'd hear me wheezing at ten yards."

That was true enough. There was a good reason Dex was our five-a-side goalkeeper. Reluctantly, I submitted to his plan.

Slinking to the Stone was easy, although it still made my heart pound. Now we're all separated. Easy pickings for a sadistic clown. I should have said something, but when nobody listens, why bother? I once read that disasters aren't made with one huge mistake, but a series of small, poor decisions. I bet there was someone who disagreed with all those choices too, but never said anything.

I don't dare peek around the Stone, as it's lit like a beacon. When Dex creates the distraction, it will be safe to look, as Scott will be facing the other way. The Stone feels hot. I'm too old for magic, but there is something special about the King Stone. Everything it's seen, over hundreds of years. The secret lovers' trysts, generations of children hurling snowballs, countless storms weathered in silence, maybe a fox slipping past at dawn with a chicken swinging from its jaws. I wonder if the King would make different choices given a second chance, and how a King decides what advice to follow, when everyone is trying to influence him. I wonder if being trapped here was a curse, or a blessing.

I hear the crazed-laugh. Even though I know it's Dex, my heart stops for a beat. The light has vanished, suddenly, and I spin around the rock to see Scott's silhouette against the menacing sky. He's looking in the wrong direction as I tear towards him, and I dive forward, targeting his soft midriff. Given my pace and gravitational advantage, I expect to blast him backwards down the grass bank. The moment before I hit, something flashes, like a star, a jewel, or the tip of a blade.

We tumble down the hill, the impact smashing all air from my lungs. I slide to a halt on the damp grass, my head lower than my feet. Everything hurts. Scott's a few feet away, his head at my chest height, and feet angled to one side. He swears. Dex jogs towards us, wheezing, and shuffling with his odd way of running.

"Gotya!" he laughs, in his high-pitched chuckle.

I try to sit but it hurts. Dex flips the switch on his torch, and we need it now. He shines it on Scott's face.

"All the gods," Dex says, and the change of tone in his voice scares me.

He shines the torch on the grass between us. It's red and slick with blood. I look at my jacket, and there's a patch of wet. Gingerly, I dab at the spot with one hand, while Dex points the torch. The blood wipes away, and Scott groans again. Dex swings the torchlight to Scott and there's a knife stuck into his thigh, with an inch of blade poking out.

"What the..." Dex keeps the beam on the knife. Scott's hands appear in the spotlight, circling the wound. I push on to my hands and knees, checking every bump and future bruise, even as my eyes stay fixed on Scott's leg and the knife.

"It's my bayonet," Scott says. "I thought I saw something, by the King."

"I told you guys, no weapons..." I say.

"Can you walk?" Dex asks. Scott shakes his head.

"Should we pull it out?" I suggest.

"No!" Scott yells.

Dex pulls me to my feet and murmurs under his breath, *he's going into shock*.

I take my iPhone out of a pocket, relieved to see the screen is still in one piece. "Hey Siri," I say. "Should I pull a knife out of a leg wound?"

There's a long pause, and it becomes obvious I have no reception. Dex checks his phone too, but we're on the same network.

"We'll carry you home," Dex decides. He grabs Scott under the arms, and indicates I should take the feet. When I grasp his ankles, Scott emits a burst of profanity, but doesn't fight us, so we stagger towards the Stone. We nearly drop him at the top, because we're knackered.

"Too many friggin' burgers," Dex says.

I think he means Scott, but it could easily be a reference to his own physique and lifestyle choices.

"We're never gonna make it down the hill," I say. "One of us should get help, while the other stays with him."

"You get the help. I'll wait here," Dex says.

"I'm not dead yet," Scott comments, but doesn't give us any other hints on what to do.

As the oldest by at least a couple of decades, Dex is our unspoken leader. He's the most experienced, he's done things I haven't even imagined, like two divorces. We all do the same role, but he's the shift leader. Sometimes though, I wonder why we listen to his advice, when he seems to have made such a mess of things.

"Chop, chop," he says. I know there's little point in arguing.

"No," I tell him, surprising myself.

Despite his permanent smile, high-pitched laugh and easy-going attitude, he can switch on an evil stare. I endure the full power of it now. He locks his eyes on mine.

"They live in the pond," Scott says softly.

I look at him lying there, and consider if he's turning delirious.

"Who does, Scott?" I ask.

"Snails. They can survive in water."

"That's fresh water," Dex says and shakes his head. He turns, and shielding his body from the strengthening wind, lights a cigarette.

"Give me your jacket," I say to Dex.

Meekly, he hands the cigarette to Scott, peels the jacket off, and lays it over him, then looks down at Scott for a moment.

"Try not to bleed on it," he says.

"Tell them to bring the ambulance there," I point to the main road.

He shrugs, and without another word, saunters off towards the estate.

"Be quick!" I shout after him.

He lifts a two-fingered salute over his shoulder and disappears down the slope.

"Thanks, by the way," I say to Scott.

"For not gutting you?"

"Yep."

"Did you know it was me?" I ask him, but he doesn't reply.

We sit there for a minute, lost in silence.

"What happened to the witch," Scott says.

I pause. "Didn't she turn into a white hare - what was that phrase? *She zig-zagged over the hill and was gone.*"

"And the clown?" Scott asks.

"You mean the jester?" I correct him.

"Same thing," he says.

I shake my head. It feels cold and exposed on the hill.

Scott sucks in a breath, "Who comes up with this shit?"

There's something in his voice though, a trace of fear. Unless it's the pain.

"If you lean on me, do you think you could hop downhill?" I ask Scott.

"I can try. Shouldn't we wait for Dex and the cavalry?"

"Let's meet them halfway," I say.

The first portion down the steep part of the slope is tricky. We take a long time. Once we get into a rhythm, we start to do better, and Scott grits his teeth before each swinging step. At the corner of the field I prop him against a fence-post while I pick at the rope-knot looped around the gate's latch.

Scott sticks both hands into his pockets to keep warm, shivering badly. Then he begins to swear, quietly and repeatedly. I turn. He holds out a bedraggled, shapeless bunch of fur and skin and waits for a reaction. My brain pieces the puzzle together. It's a mask, a grubby clown mask. Scott looks at the pocket of the coat he's wearing, pulling my eyes to it. The coat that Dex left him.

I touch the mask with one finger and thumb, and rub them together. It feels like old leather, a rabbit skin, or a hare.

At the bottom of the next field I see flashing hazard lights.

"Is that the ambulance?" Scott says.

"No, it's his car."

Between the strobing lights, I make out the broad figure of Dex shuffling up the hill towards us. He's carrying something, maybe the poles of a rolled-up stretcher, or is that a shovel?

"Put it back in his pocket," I say.

Scott looks me in the eye, and I'm not sure who's the most frightened. For once though, he takes my advice. He says, "If you need my bayonet, take it."

"Do you know any good jokes?" I say.

"I'm not the jester in this pack," he tells me.

Dex is closer, his shambling figure getting bigger with each step.

"Knock, knock," I whisper.

"Who's there?"

"Cash."

Scott gulps. "Cash who?"

"Yep, we've got a real nut coming."

It's not that funny, but Scot laughs. I knock on wood.

Michael Gaspeny

Farewell, Globed Fruit

A poem should be palpable and mute
As a globed fruit-- Archibald MacLeish, *Ars Poetica*

During my last visit to you, buddy since high school,
I learned how it feels to be "in stir," the bars, pedagoguery.
You gave me assignments—"Watch this video
about Eero Saarinen by his son, a poignant illustration
of filial love. I'll be on the phone. By the way,
this exquisite short story by Michael Martone
will keep you busy. We shall discuss."
Pal of fifty-five years, talking syllabus

and warden: "Don't leave a crack in the blinds.
I like lounging at the table in my skivvies while I stroke
the cats, which, incidentally, must stay in the basement
at night. Otherwise, their restlessness keeps me awake."
We quibbled over who directed which picture
or hit .341 in 1910. My stay—a trivia game.
Remember when we talked about life?

On the fourth day, while you napped, I flipped through
an anthology, stopping on Neruda's "I Have a Few Things
To Explain," a furious poem about 1936 in Madrid
when Franco's bastards blasted the poet's neighborhood
and olive oil and children's blood splashed the cobbles.
Neruda said to readers: Forget the beauty you expect
until we avenge the slaughtered.

His fire inspired me. I raised the blinds and a Miller 40.
Across the alley, wind shook the cypresses as if it blew

from Neruda. Forsaking all that was "mute,"
I wanted to roar at my friend, Archibald MacLeish,
and, most of all, me—"No more cages!"

John Sibley Williams

A History of Skin

I've played out the Cowboy/Indian
narrative by myself in dark wooded
corners where trees hold each other
so damn tight the sky erases itself. I
remember beating my t-shirt against
rocks to get the blood out, how dirt
brown the stains set, how stone isn't
the best salve. Turn a switch around
& spear becomes rifle, son turns to
man. *Please bury me like this*, I said to
no one who could hear me. Gray as
bathwater, as the palette between
skins, one not really mine, the light
passed through a thousand branches
before failing to find me. I opened &
closed. If every good story begins
with a lie, this is mine: once a boy
who played both sides of slaughter
returned home with a bloody shirt &
thought that would absolve him.

Sam Anderson

The Only Rule that Matters

At WE-SAVE grocery, when you got trained to be a cashier, you had to watch this awful video about how stealing is wrong. I don't mean that I thought stealing was right, just that everyone at the store seemed to know there were no cameras beyond the check lanes. Everyone at that dump helped themselves to free food during shifts when nobody looked. The video was awful in the sense that the actors took their roles in it way too seriously and ended up creating something that I couldn't help but roll my eyes at.

I leaned back in the crappy plastic chair and counted the pinpoint holes in the ceiling tiles. I'd had to watch this video when I first started as a stock clerk, and the check lane supervisor, Sharon, said I had to watch it again as a refresher. She laughed when she said it, but her eyes told me that I'd better sit through the thing. There was only one other person in the break room with me. Vicki, a cute girl who had painted little white crosses on her thumbnails, dutifully took notes and seemed to miss how funny the video really was. Mostly I spent the time trying not to get caught checking her out.

"You should sit up," she said. "Sharon said we have a test after this."

"I've taken it already. The right answers will be A, A, B, C, and A."

Vicki glanced sidelong toward me, scowled, and shook her head. "Great, now I missed what that guy just said."

I just slouched down further into my chair and went through my list of chores for the day.

The overhead speaker clicked to life and called for a clerk to aisle one for a clean-up. That was my cue. Condiments aisle. Would it be ketchup, mustard, or jelly all over the floor? Mop needed any way it went. I told Vicki that I had to step out and she promised to share her notes with me when I got back. I did my best not to chortle but I'm pretty sure she heard me.

I found aisle one's tiles virtually pristine when I got there. With the mop in hand, I walked slowly up and down along the shelves, half-crouched trying to catch a change in the way a tile shined. By the time I made my third loop back down the aisle, I looked up to see Tallywacker – that's what we all called Gabe Teluwick, the store manager – with his arms crossed and the purple vein in his forehead bulging. He stomped toward me and said, "Mr. Winsel, what do you think you are doing in this aisle? There's dog food all over aisle ten."

"You said aisle one."

That only made Gabe glare harder at me. "No, you must have heard wrong. I clearly said dog food spill in aisle ten. If I ever took a day off, this store would fall apart." He ranted like that for a good minute before he finally told me to take the mop bucket back and dump it out. "Might have to take the cost of that soap out of your next paycheck," he said. Gabe shook his head, and nearly ran Sharon over when he turned back toward the front check lanes.

"Gabe, sweetheart, are you torturing Cameron?" Sharon crooked an eyebrow up at Gabe. When he saw me smiling, Gabe shooed me away. The last thing I heard her say before I left the aisle was, "Cameron's training on register. He's off limits."

That was the great secret of WE-SAVE: Gabe thought he had the power, but really all he did was hover up by the check lanes and lord over everyone with his nose up in the air. Sharon and Ted, the assistant managers, kept the store from falling apart. Ted missed his days spent as a clerk and so he preferred to work alongside me every shift we had together. He'd reminisce about his old rainbow mohawk that Gabe made him shave off, and the time he managed to fit forty-four carts on the broken-down old electric caddy.

Sharon, though, was crafty. She watched the monitors in the managerial office and learned. Gabe may have thought he was a king of the store, but Sharon was the queen. She let Gabe think that he controlled everything, but it was her eyes and ears that kept the rest of us goons in line. The last thing any of us wanted to see was Sharon's curled black hair and cream polo charging down the length of the lanes toward us.

Once, a couple weeks before, a girl tried to pocket a twenty-dollar bill. Sharon must have been watching on the monitors in her office because she threw open the door and pointed right at lane 6. I was pulling carts in from the parking lot when it happened, and even above the roar of the electric cart caddy I could hear Sharon's voice sink into the girl. "You! My office! Now!" Those were the words that nobody wanted to hear. Even with a row of carts between Sharon and me, the simple phrase made the hairs on my arms stand on end. The girl was fired on the spot. She kicked a cart out of her way on the way to her car, and I had to chase it down the hill of our parking lot before it rolled out into the street.

Only once did Tallywacker try to openly accuse Sharon of stealing from a register. My drawer during one shift had come back short about five dollars. Tallywacker threw a fit up by the office, red-faced and spittle-lipped. I stood there quietly beside Sharon while Gabe raged on. Vicki glanced over at me from a nearby check lane and tried to look like she wasn't paying attention.

From beside me, I clued in to the conversation, "and you were the one who checked in Cameron's drawer?" Gabe's fingers squeezed the edge of the register.

"I hadn't gotten around to it, just yet. I've been busy. If you hadn't noticed, we have a sale going on right now." Sharon winked up at him, and with one hand behind her back, gestured for me to wander off. And like that, the issue was dropped.

A few shifts later I was sitting at a deli table off in the corner of the store when Sharon walked by. I had my forehead against the Formica and let my hair spread out in all directions while I rubbed the back of my neck. My stomach hurt because I couldn't even afford to eat. I had about thirty-seven cents in my pocket and my roommate told me that he was done buying me food. I'd been living on scavenged junk food for the past three days while hiding in the back warehouse, but my stomach was ripping itself apart. This was late in my shift. It was so dark you couldn't see anything but headlights through the front windows.

Sharon sat at the seat in front of me and said, "This job isn't *that* bad." She rubbed my shoulder while she spoke, and before I lifted my head I could have sworn my mother was the one trying to comfort me. Now that I think about it, she had green eyes just like Mom.

My stomach rumbled then, and she asked me if I'd eaten. I shook my head and without another word she stood up and went into the deli kitchen.

She and the deli cook had a heated discussion, then both craned their necks out the door toward the front registers where Gabe stood. Sharon said, a little louder now, "Girl, you know you just have to dump this in the trash chute, anyway. Let Cameron do it for you. Who cares if he eats some of the food on the way back?" Sharon told me there were no cameras back by the trash compactor, and as long as I didn't mind the smell of garbage then nobody would know.

"Ten to one says the boy screws this up and gets Gabe up my ass." The deli cook wheeled a little black cart with containers of old heat lamp food all over it. Sharon told her not to worry about it and that Gabe was too busy shoving sticks up his own ass most days.

Five minutes later, I was pushing a cart full of cold chicken and warm potato salad back to the trash chute. That's just the sort of person Sharon was: she took care of everyone, even if they didn't ask for help.

Mostly I clerked – ran price checks, filled the shelves, cleaned crap off bathroom floors among other delightful chores – but on the weekends when things got crazy at the registers, Sharon would call me up to the front to help thin out the growing lines of shoppers that slowly merged into a mob. I hated standing still for so long listening to *beep* after *beep* after *beep*. And customers would always wait until that very moment that I hit "confirm" after the final moment to remember they had fifty coupons for half of their items. But, hey, Sharon made me want to deal with all of that nonsense.

One woman once had twenty-three coupons that she remembered only after I'd put her cash into the register.

"Oh, hell no, wait. That's not right," she said when the total came up. When I refused to void the order and start scanning all her items over again, she clicked her fingers toward Gabe who started over. Sharon stepped in between him and my register and shut off my light.

"What seems to be the problem, ma'am?" Sharon pulled me to the side and folded her hands in front of her.

The woman waved her wad of coupons toward me. "This idiot here refused—"

Sharon cleared her throat and smiled back. "Politeness earns points. Don't be rude."

The woman's eyes went wide, then she glared at Sharon, who stood upright and stoic. At last, she raised her folded hands and said, "Now, if you're ready to try again, let me take you over to Customer Service and we can ring you up with those coupons." Sharon hit the Void key on the register before the woman could respond. Before I could tell the woman what to do with her coupons, Sharon put the bagged groceries into the woman's cart and helped her over to the service counter.

Thankfully, a sick kid puked over by paper plates and Gabe told me to go take care of it. I drew the magnetic chain across the lane's belt before any other customers could put their items down.

On the Fourth of July, every lane was packed with lines reaching into the aisles. Sharon was cashiering at the lane in front of mine. I was on Lane 4, she had Lane 5. The big sale items of the day were giant bags of ice, thirty-pack cases of beer, and charcoal. As much as I usually hated to work the cash registers, the ice soothed my fingers where the metal carts from outside had burnt lines into the skin.

"Thanks for shopping at WE-SAVE, where you save when we save!" I said to a tired man holding a baby in his arms. I looked down to realize I was passing condoms over the lasers, then a loaf of bread, then some butter and milk, and finally a coloring book with some crayons on it. I stared at the crayons in one hand and condoms in the other. I must have looked confused because the man in front of me laughed and just said, "Kids, man."

His smile looked defeated, a twitch away from a frown. The kid in his arms grabbed the man's beard in both hands and pulled in opposite directions. When he looked with a sigh at the jumble of items at the end of the lane, I stepped away from the register and started putting everything into a paper bag for him.

I glanced over at Sharon and sticking out of her back pocket was the corner of a folded twenty-dollar bill. Her register was wide open, and she was laughing along to a joke the guy buying a pack of beer was telling. She reached out and handed the guy his change, and after he walked off, she went to close her drawer, slipped a dollar bill out over the edge, and slid her hand into the back pocket of her jeans, stuffing the cash down farther. The man in front of me cleared his throat and asked if I was going to just stare at her ass all day or finish bagging his groceries. He thumbed through cash in his wallet and set several bills on the scanner.

When Sharon looked over, I was standing beside the paper sack with the box of condoms held up above it. Sharon just said, "Cam, I'm too old for you." She winked at me. I suddenly became aware of my sunburnt cheeks and stuffed the rest of the man's items into the sack. I handed him back his change and thanked him for shopping at WE-SAVE.

Gabe appeared beside my open register with a roll of paper towels and a spray bottle of the cheap, watered-down cleaner. He stared down his long nose at the cash in the drawer and reminded me that when I was done, the bathrooms looked like nobody had cleaned them yet. Which sucked, because I had just gotten done with them before I hopped on the lane. Gabe pushed the open register drawer closed with the paper towels and said, "Don't leave your register open like that. Sharon hates a light drawer." I looked her way, and she wouldn't meet my eyes. I wondered, briefly, if I should tell him about what I'd seen.

Gabe shoved the cleaning supplies into my hands and said

that my clerking expertise was needed urgently and that he would finish up for me. He said this, staring intently at Sharon the entire time. Did he already know?

When he stepped up to my register, Sharon turned around and said, "Gabe, sweetie, we're almost cleared out. We don't really need the extra help. I'm sure you've got more important things to do, anyway. This place would fall apart without you taking care of it." She looked like she might gag, but Gabe seemed to buy it. He rubbed his fingers along the end of his nose, then nodded. "I'll just balance out his drawer, then."

"I can do it, I'm about to cash out my drawer anyway." She switched off her light. Sharon popped her register open and came over. Gabe seemed happy. He looked over at me and told me that the carts would need to be run in after I was done with the restrooms.

I got back in from that cart run, and saw Sharon walking back toward the break room through the aisles. When she was out of view of the cameras, she reached into the pocket I'd seen the cash in before and pulled out a jumble of bills. She tapped the bills into a neat little stack, folded it, and slid it back into the pocket. Curiosity took over and I wondered what she did with any money she took. Had any of the other cashiers who she caught stealing been stealing? Ted and I were prone to the occasional "broken beer" in the dairy cooler, but taking money seemed like something else entirely.

A little kid in a cart waved at her near the end of the JELL-O cups, and she waved back, making cooing noises at him. The boy stuck his tongue out at me when I passed a few seconds later. When I stuck my tongue out at him, his mother glared at me. "Thanks for shopping at WE-SAVE!" I gave her two thumbs up and kept walking.

I followed Sharon through the rear doors into the stock room, past the pallets of cheap beer and charcoal. When she entered the break room, I waited around the corner for a few seconds, so it wouldn't seem suspicious if I came in right after her. I heard a locker creak open, then close. I waited for a few seconds and ducked around the corner into the door. She pulled money out of her purse when I entered. She added the new bills to a thick money clip with the bills folded in half. I bumped into the trash can beside the door and she twirled around, eyes wide. "Jesus, you can't just sneak up on people!" She must have noticed me staring at the cash, because she slipped it back into the purse and put it on the chair beside her. "You here to rob me, or something?"

I sat in the chair across from her and asked her, "How long?"

"What?"

"How long have you been taking out of your register?"

Sharon looked down at the purse and tapped her fingers on the table. After several seconds she said, "I don't know what you're talking about."

"Look, I saw you earlier."

"And what did you see?"

I told her I'd seen her pull money out of the register. Then I asked, "Why? Don't you get paid manager money or something?" She just laughed and said that I had a lot of growing up to do. "We all got our secrets here, Cam. If Gabe knew half of the things we did around here, we'd probably all get fired. You gotta take care of yourself. This place sure as hell don't take care of any of us."

"Okay, yeah, I get that. But doesn't that hurt everyone here?"

"Listen to yourself. You plan on staying here your whole life? You one of these Grocery Manager-for-Lifers?"

The look on her face made me sink back a little.

"Cameron, honey. Don't be Gabe. Don't just take what is given to you." Her words echoed something my mother had told me shortly before leaving Dad. *Sometimes, life deals you a shitty hand and you have to shuffle the cards while the dealer isn't looking.* I couldn't understand it then, but something in what Sharon said seemed to make sense.

"So, what do we do from here, then?"

She grabbed my hands and pulled them toward her. We sat like that, hands clasped in the center of the table and leaning on our elbows, for several seconds. She dug her nails into my palms. "*We* do nothing. Who do you think Gabe would believe, anyway? His check lane supervisor, or a new-hire clerk who gets caught stealing deli food on the clock?"

My stomach lurched. "I thought we couldn't sell that food."

"To customers. You think Gabe would say no to *you* buying it?"

"Fine, I'll keep my mouth shut." She let go. Tiny crescent marks lingered along the edge of my hand where her nails had pressed into the skin. I walked back out to the main floor. Over the intercom, Ted called for me to get a mop and head to the baked goods aisle to clean up a sugar spill.

The thing about sugar spills on white tile is that you can never be certain you've completely cleaned up the mess until hours later when there are gray streaks up and down the aisle. Ted pushed me back into the aisle later and scraped his shoe along the gray streaks and explained that I hadn't swept enough of the sugar up before mopping. According to him, this was probably going to take the rest of my shift to clean up. He told me to get another mop bucket and spend however long it took to fix this.

What he didn't bother to tell me was that if I didn't block off the aisle while I worked, the new wet tiles would cause the streaks to stretch out into other aisles when customers rolled through. By the end of the first hour, the next two aisles were also gray. After two hours, most of the aisles were dirty. I watched in slow motion as each time I finished mopping an aisle, the streaks seemed to stretch farther out, toward Produce on one end of the store, weaving in between the vegetable bunkers, around toward the Deli up front, eventually leaving dingy streaks near the registers.

By the fourth hour mopping, each new section I cleaned became dingy all over again. My biceps felt like they would give out if I kept lifting the mop into the bucket, and each swish of the mop felt like it might break my arms. By the fifth hour, I realized that I was leaving size 9 gray footprints wherever I walked.

I threw the mop down when Ted found me back by the soda aisle. I told him that my arms were too sore to keep mopping and that the aisles were grayer than when I started, Ted started laughing and said, "Yeah, I know. The floor crew will fix it tonight. That's why we pay them."

"Then why did you have me mop this up?"

He shrugged once, stuck out his lower lip, and just said, "Boredom." He nodded once, then added, "Plus, I wanted to see how long I could keep you going before Gabe got pissed that we were out of carts up front. You should see how purple his forehead is."

I rubbed at my eyes with both palms. "I don't think I can push carts in right now."

"Fine, I'll help you, but I get to call you a baby for the rest of the night."

He wasn't lying. There were roughly a dozen or so carts left up front for customers and most of the corrals out front were filled. Even working together with the electronic caddy, it took Ted and me most of an hour to fill the bay again. While we pushed carts up the hill, something kept gnawing at my gut. The tiny crescents were gone, but I swore I could still feel them.

"So, you know how we all basically just sort of... help ourselves?" I pulled three carts onto the caddy.

Ted looked confused. "God, I'm helping you right now, you big baby."

"No, I mean like, when a beer bottle "breaks" and we're supposed to dump the other five."

"Oh, Jesus. Don't go all Beaver Cleaver on me. What about it?"

"Where exactly is the line?"

Ted stopped pushing for a moment and stared hard at me. He squinted, peering through his brows at me in a way that made me feel naked. "Stealing is stealing, right? That's what Gabe would say."

"What do you say?"

"Take whatever you need and the rest sorts itself out. Corporate pays for damaged goods, after all. Or, sometimes just empty chicken finger containers make it down the trash chute."

I tried to look surprised. "What does that mean?"

"What, you think you're the first clerk to get the deli special?"

"Why are you telling me this?"

Ted's lower jaw jutted forward more, and his furrowed brow made him look like a cave man. "So you get smarter about it."

"What?"

"I was curious how long before you would catch on to the free food. Just don't let Gabe catch you. Stealing's the only way to get fired, really."

"Aren't you supposed to report to him since you're the assistant manager?"

He laughed.

"What about if I know someone who's actually stealing? Not just food but money from the checkout lanes."

"Talk to Sharon."

I must have made a face because Ted's eyes widened, and he nodded. "First two rules of survival here at WE-SAVE: look out for yourself, and don't be Gabe's lap dog."

"But what about—?"

He held his hands to his ears. "I think you can handle the rest of these carts." The cart he was pushing started to roll down the hill. He told me that I better get it before it hit a car or an old lady or something.

By the time I got back in from finishing that cart run, I had an hour left on my shift. I brushed off the dust from outside and lumbered toward the stock room. If I could stay out of sight for the last hour, then all the messes and empty spots on shelves would be the night shift's problem. Vicki was alone in the break room, and I sat down at the table next to hers. She rooted through her purse with a frown on her face. The pout just made her cuter.

"What's wrong?" I asked. I leaned my head back and pretended to count the holes in the ceiling tiles.

"I swear I had a few dollars in my purse earlier. Maybe I spent it."

I looked over and realized that the purse she had in front of her was the same one that Sharon had been going through when I caught her before. "Did you lock your locker?"

"Of course." She rolled her eyes. As she dug through the purse, though, she pulled a lock out of it. She looked surprised to see it, then glanced over at the locker. "Or maybe I didn't?"

I wanted to lean over and tell her, suavely, that this place was a den of scum and villainy like Mos Eisley, but what came out was, "Freaking rats, man."

She wrinkled her nose at me and shook her head. "I should tell Gabe about this."

"He won't do anything." I pointed to the sign above the lockers that said, in all caps: *MANAGEMENT AND WE-SAVE ARE NOT RESPONSIBLE FOR LOSS OR THEFT OF PERSONAL PROPERTY.*

Vicki's eyes were getting wet. "Well, somebody should say something."

Something inside me broke for a moment. "I think I saw... no, never mind."

"What?"

"I thought I saw Sharon back here. Maybe she saw somebody with your purse?"

Vicki said she'd check with Sharon and walked out. I promptly set the alarm on my phone and pressed my cheek into the cold bench of the booth.

Later in the week, while pushing carts in from the lot, I saw Sharon dragging Vicki over to Gabe's door. He stood silently while Sharon accused the girl of stealing money. Her drawer had come up almost $100 short. I slid the carts into their spot in the front bay and crept closer. Sharon saw me standing beside the carts watching. Her eyes narrowed.

Gabe's face turned red, and the purple vein in his forehead bulged. He held out a hand and said, "Name badge, Vicki. This is unacceptable. God, I think I'm going to have to file a report with the police for this amount."

Sharon looked smug.

Vicki's mascara was beginning to smear. "I don't know why my drawer was short, I swear I don't! I double-checked it before returning it, like the video told me to. It was full when I turned it in! I mean first the money from my purse and now this, I—"

Gabe clicked his tongue, told her not to make excuses for her actions, and held his open palm out farther. Vicki put the badge in his hand, and Sharon escorted her into the office and closed the door. When he saw me standing around, he shook his head and said, "Always a shame when you thought you could trust someone, you know?" He turned to enter his own office, and I followed him inside.

He looked up from his desk when I entered. "Can I help you, Cameron?"

Vicki didn't strike me as the kind of girl who would rob anyone. From the few times I talked with her, I learned she was a minister's daughter, working for the summer so she could save up to help pay for a car. She was probably the nicest person in this place, and I suspected she might be the only one *not* stealing from the store. "I don't think Vicki stole that money."

"Do you have proof?"

"No, but who checks the registers after shifts?"

"Sharon." He leaned forward, suddenly interested. "You know something I don't?"

I thought about telling him what I'd seen on the Fourth of July. That she'd pocketed cash from a drawer. But, that felt too greasy. I heard Ted recounting the rules of WE-SAVE survival and didn't think I could face his wrath by turning full rat. But, at the same time, she had stolen money from Vicki, which crossed a whole other line. Gabe cleared his throat looked down at his watch. "Can we move this along, Mr. Winsel?"

Instead, I asked, "Does anyone *else* ever check on the drawers after Sharon closes out shifts? I know Vicki had some money taken out of her locker the other day. Somebody here seems to be stealing from employees." Gabe scratched his chin and stared at his desk for several seconds. He nodded and thanked me for the information.

The next day, when I reached the trash chute with the deli cart, I found Gabe standing beside the open chute. He glowered at me as I walked up and leaned in close. He whispered that I had some potato salad on my shirt. His gaze dropped to the cart, on the half-eaten potato salad with the fork sticking out of it. "This is your only warning. I'm disappointed in you."

Sharon was fired later that week and wouldn't look at me when she passed by on the way out the front doors. She looked strange without the cream WE-SAVE polo on, like a queen without her crown. Gabe practically glowed up by the registers when he told me he'd found the thief thanks to me. I cringed as everyone turned to see who Gabe was speaking to. Ted found more and more excuses and cleanups to keep me on my feet all shift long and refused to help while working like he had before. When I asked him why, he said I'd broken the only rule that mattered. Then he turned toward me, smiled, and pushed a bag of sugar off the shelf, between us.

Sam Love

Ballet Mechanistic

Like a choreographed dance
the gunmetal arms swing
rotate, lift and swoosh
following targets of laser eyes
plotting points X, Y and Z

Spraying, welding, machining
with precise moves once done by humans
the robots swing back and forth
and are never bored, never demand a break
or walk the picket line

Complete with opposable claws
flexible elbows and pressure sensors
they position components
with a delicate touch
more consistent than a human

With the ability to mimic
movements on an assembly line
that worships repetitive motion
workers can train the robot to take
their job just by matching their moves

As the robots go through their fluid ballet
one has to wonder if their chipped brains
are simply commanding movements
or if they dream of a self-replicating world
freed from human commands

Jonathan Greenhause

I set out to write

nothing
about nothing. Online,
bloggers
pen crowded verses about
loneliness,

about how silence becomes
a disease
afflicting the tongue. Birds
tweet
about celebrity birds

but neglect
to admire the puffy clouds
through which
they plummet. Life becomes
a joke

on all of us. Meanwhile,
Facebook
commissions poets
to create
poems about Facebook.

There's
nothing I could say
better
than nothing. So I shut
the fuck up,

let my pregnant pauses
                    gestate
into a white room with
                    an elephant.
I become the endangered

                    forest
burnt to a crisp by well-
                    intentioned
arsonists. I'm anaphoric
                    but fear

repetition, set out
                    on foot
but regress into a series of
                    handstands.
Asked for my birthdate

                    I hear
"first date" & proceed
                    to feel
embarrassed. No one even
                    kissed me

'til it was way too late.
                    "No one"
is another way of saying
                    my first wife
from whom I'm happily

estranged.
It's strange to think about
anything,
bizarre to be able to decide
not to, too.

I set out to write something
about some-
thing, wind up with
an expanse
of snow disguised as

a blank
sheet of soaked paper.

Grace Ellis

OUT IN THE YARD

In 1953 my family moved from Virginia to Tuscaloosa, Alabama. Our white frame house there, with the layout of a typical mill house, had been moved from another site, and a large kitchen had been added on, along with a bedroom to accommodate bunk beds for my three brothers. I was seven years old, my brother James was six, and our twin brothers, Rannie and Bruce, were two-year-old toddlers. We lived in that house for seven years as we began to grow up. But much of our life took place in the various parts of the yard that surrounded it.

The front yard was small. The house had a front porch and steps leading down to a sidewalk, which led to a street. Actually, the street was a highway, US 11, a major thoroughfare in those pre-interstate years. Across the highway was the campus of Stillman College where my father taught. It was my job to sweep the front porch and the sidewalk. Often I would take a piece of chalk and draw a design for hopscotch on the sidewalk. I had learned to play the game with friends at school, but at home I mostly played by myself. My brothers were not interested in that pastime.

At the other end of the house was a small back porch—what people called a "stoop"—a concrete square with a larger square beneath it, and then the ground. The back yard, larger than the one in front of the house, was surrounded by a hedge. When my brother James and I were learning to ride our bikes without training wheels, we would each pull our bike up next to the porch, swing a leg over and coast into the hedge, which gave us a relatively soft landing until we learned how to use the brakes.

The back yard had room for a clothes line, where our mother could hang sheets and towels and garments to dry in the fresh air. Over the years of my adult life, I have usually managed to live in a place where I could string up a clothes line to use on sunny days. I have one still.

As we grew older, I used to participate in my brothers' football scrimmages in the back yard, sometimes including the two boys who lived next door. My role was usually to hand off the football and then get out of their way. But I learned some of the basic rules and vocabulary of football—a great advantage when, in high school and later in college, I would be invited to attend football games and be expected to grasp what was happening on the field.

To the side of our house was a large vacant lot that we children claimed as our own. At the back of the lot was a huge oak tree. Strips of wood were nailed to the big trunk, and we used them to ascend into the branches. I was generally unathletic, but I became skillful at climbing from branch to branch, higher and higher, until I peered down through the leaves at the ground far below. We climbed so high that we would have done considerable damage to ourselves if we had fallen, but, fortunately, we never did.

Underneath the tree was a swing set with two swings and a "sky scooter," which might as well have been designed for twins. In our early years in Tuscaloosa, Bruce and Rannie used to spend hours on the sky scooter, pumping in prefect rhythm as it moved back and forth.

In the area between US 11 and the side street was a grassy field. I learned the contours of the field well, because when I was old enough, I used to take my turn mowing it with a push mower. My father taught me to make long straight lines that formed a rectangle, which became smaller and smaller until I reached the center and all the tall grass was gone. This activity was boring but soothing for me—as I slowly made progress, watching the size of my task diminish.

In the corner next to the side street and furthest from the oak tree was a shallow indentation about seven feet long and five feet wide. We called it "the pit." After one summer in Richmond, Virginia, where we stayed in an apartment complex and learned the ways of unsupervised groups of children, my three brothers formed a club. One of its purposes was to gang up and push me into the pit. I didn't give my brothers the satisfaction of being terrorized by this behavior. After all, the pit wasn't deep at all, and I could easily just walk out of it. But our disapproving parents decided to outlaw clubs. So my brothers re-branded themselves as "The Eee-Yaah Friendship Group," which was still devoted to harassing me. Years later, after my father's death, I would receive a generous gift from my brothers, with a card signed "The Eee-Yaah Friendship Group."

I visited Tuscaloosa several years ago and discovered that our house is gone. And the giant oak tree. And the elementary school at the end of the block. All laid bare by progress. Perhaps the house was knocked down, or perhaps a truck came and moved it again, to a new environment. But the yard that surrounded it from 1953 to 1960 still exists in my memory—and occasionally in my dreams.

Michael Kocinski

Little Love Song

"No deaths or separations, no disappointments in love."
Jane Kenyon, American Triptych, Part: 2 Down the Road

My beautiful wife and
our babies are in Nashville,
singing and dancing
like a bunch of catbirds
in the bustling woods.

I slept in until 10 am,
didn't have to make
breakfast for anybody
or negotiate inevitably
broken treaties between my sons,
who are like two countries
at war over disputed territory.

I do the dishes
while listening to 'Kind of Blue'.
Outside the kitchen window
the clouded sulphurs
cartwheel in the alfalfa,
mating and laying eggs.
They lace mud puddles
in the gravel driveway,
sipping salt and other
minerals all animals need
to thrive.

There's a potato stinking
in the pantry and a fly buzzing
around the garbage can--
not everything is perfect,
but it's very close.

I feel like I'm in the middle
of a Jane Kenyon poem,
one of those bittersweet
meditations in the middle
of the farmyard,
watching my beloved
chop wood or bale hay,
wringing a towel
in my hands after
rinsing and drying the dishes,
knowing the sun will set
on all of this day,
not certain I'll see it rise,
not certain any of us
will see it rise,

But oh, look--
my wife has seen me
standing in the yard.
She waves, she smiles,
the sky is golden.

David Radavich

DOWNSIZING

What will live
in a smaller space?

The rooms you
can fold up
and put
in your pick-up,

give away
the rest
to the wandering
homeless.

I will never be
more svelte

than this house
with its
lost interiors.

Time echoes
giving walls ears.

Come take us
away like a jewel

that has moved
on this hand
this many morns.

Steve Cushman

Snakebit

Guy Wilson was straightening up a stack of wood, out back behind his shed, when he felt the quick pinch in the palm of his hand. Guy shook his hand and the small brown snake slithered back to its hiding place behind the wood.

Guy walked slowly to his porch and sat in a lawn chair, surveyed his hand and the two small puncture wounds, each pink now with a slightly red core. His heart quickened as he waited for something to happen, for dizziness, for swelling, but nothing did, so he leaned back and closed his eyes, told himself to relax, as he felt this sunny spring Sunday morning on his face.

He wondered if his hand would grow thick with swelling, if he'd be dead in a few hours. He wondered if it would simply heal without treatment. He knew little about snakes and didn't know if this one was poisonous or not. It was brown with lines circling its body. Guy considered going to the hospital, but didn't see the point. He hadn't been to the doctor in thirty-three years and had no intention of starting now.

He considered calling Sara, his ex-wife, or his son, Wes, but he spoke to both of them so infrequently he didn't know what he'd say. Conversations with his son were always so damn uncomfortable. He'd wanted to have the sort of father-son relationship where they sat on the back porch, drinking beer, telling stories, but it never happened. Perhaps it didn't happen to anyone. Perhaps that was all TV bullshit, but he wanted to feel close, to feel loved, by this person he had helped create, shelter and shepherd through childhood. He wanted to teach him something before it was too late.

But instead of calling, Guy left his keys in the front door and set out on a walk around his neighborhood, something he couldn't remember doing since his dog, Lucy, died last year. She had been a good dog, a black lab mix. He walked her for fifteen minutes every morning and evening, the same three block-route, until one day he came home from work and found her splayed out on the kitchen floor. Her bowels had loosened, but she still wore that endearing smile of hers.

The houses he passed now all seemed nicer, bigger, than his. The grasses greener, and the cars in the driveways all had a shine he couldn't recall his own vehicle, a 17-year-old Volvo, ever possessing.

Guy knew he was going to die soon. If not today, from this snakebite, then soon. He'd not lived the life he'd wanted. Back in the distant memory of school and possible futures, he'd played clarinet and dreamed of being a high school music teacher, but his parents (a doctor and stay-at-home mom) insisted he go into computers, and being an agreeable kid he did what they said.

Now, a block from home, he heard Beethoven's *Fifth Symphony* floating out a window. Guy smiled as the piece lifted him up and down and up again. He thought of Mrs. White's band room. The feel of the clarinet in his hand, the coolness of those silver keys against the tip of his fingers.

When the song ended, Guy began to run. His knee hurt and his calf pinched but still he ran. For a few moments he was not a 59-year-old competent, senior computer programmer at McGill Wholesale but instead a teenage boy running home from school clutching his clarinet case. Sara Parker had given him her phone number, and Guy had to figure out what to say when he called her.

The grass flew by, then and now, the houses a blur, and even when he felt he could no longer breathe, still he ran, figuring this was it. Soon, it would all be over. But after circling his neighborhood twice he was not dead, only out of breath, his chest aching, his shirt wet, the pain in his hand thumping where the two red dots marked his palm.

His neighbor was out on the driveway, grilling. This family had lived beside him for at least a year, and he didn't even know their last name. They looked, to Guy, like Smiths. Each Saturday, Mr. Smith dragged his gas grill from the garage to the driveway where he grilled steaks and drank beers while the chunky daughter (about five or so) rode her yellow bike back and forth on the sidewalk in front of the house.

As Guy walked up the driveway, Mr. Smith turned and smiled. "Afternoon," the man said. He was short with slick black hair, wearing his weekend outfit of tan shorts, pink polo shirt, and flip-flops. This Smith seemed like a golfer to Guy. Golf was a sport he never saw the point of.

"What's your name?" Guy asked.

"Kevin, Kevin Wagner."

"And your wife, your daughter?"

"Kelly, and our daughter is Jessica."

"Nice," Guy said.

"Care for a beer?" Wagner asked. You could see he was trying to figure out what was happening here.

Guy shook his head. "I'm good. Just wanted to know your name."

"Now you do."

"You're right," Guy said. "I do. Do you like living here, in this neighborhood?"

Wagner flipped the steaks and steam rose between the two men.

"Sure, what's not to like?"

Guy had to admit it was a nice neighborhood. Two and three story houses with wide lawns, the occasional white columned porch. Many times driving home from work, or walking Lucy, he'd look at the well-groomed houses and think to himself *how did I end up here?* But he knew how—they'd bought the house thirty years ago with Sara's inheritance. She'd been happy to leave the house to him when she moved down to Florida to start a new life, two weeks after Wes graduated from college.

Guy could smell, almost taste, the meat on the grill, felt his heart and hand pounding. He tried to squeeze his hand, but the swelling made this impossible now.

"On second thought," he said. "I'll take one of those beers."

Wagner handed him a cold one from the garage fridge. Guy drank the beer in three long mouthfuls before handing the empty back. "Thanks," he said. "I needed that."

Back in his house, in his bedroom closet, Guy retrieved his old grey clarinet case, carried it out into the living room. He opened the windows for the breeze and turned on the CD player, cued up *The Essential Benny Goodman* and let the music fill him with a joy he had not felt in years.

Guy eased into his LA-Z-Boy and looked down to see the small pink holes on his hand had grown quarter-sized with stringy red lines extending up toward his forearm. He held the clarinet case in his lap. He hadn't tried to play it in forever, and knew he wouldn't be able to now with the swelling, but there was something comforting and painful about having it close by.

Guy felt dizzier and considered again calling Sara, but really there was nothing left to say to her. Instead, he called his son, Wes, but Wes was not home. Still, Guy was happy to hear his voice—a man now at 27—and as he listened to his son apologize for not being able to take his call Guy said the words *love, Son, love more* and then he rested the phone into its cradle and closed his eyes and Guy died.

Sandra Ann Winters

Under the Moon

My daddy built the out-of-house for us,
whitewashed the walls, cut a star in the door.
He pasted the poem "Cremation of Sam McGee"
on the wall. Stubs of candles lay in a cubby
and of course, always the bucket of lime.
I could see the moon through the star cutout,
and knew I was lucky.

The moon followed me to the sleeping porch
where I lay awake in the cooler southern air.
That cold, dry globe, studded with craters,
and strewn with rocks and dust led me through
my periodic rises and falls. I pondered
the full moon, the waning gibbous moon
and waxing crescent moon.

The moon has followed me through all my nights,
through, sleeping on the hard earth
under the Sierra and Utah skies,
through nights on the sand dunes by the Atlantic.
It has followed me through rocking on the glider
that stretches out on the screened porch.

When I pee to the glinting stars' tune,
I know my daddy was the man-in-the-moon.

Katherine Wolfe

AN ORDINARY MOTHER
In memory of my mother 1915-1962

When I was sixteen I wanted my mother
to be an ordinary stay-at-home
mom like the mothers of my friends.
I didn't like it that she slung
a Rolleiflex camera over her shoulder
and snapped photos of other mothers
who played bridge, attended teas,
or took their children to the pool
on a hot afternoon.
I didn't like it that she was always
looking for a story to tell in photos.

> *She had blue eyes, azure blue,*
> *and wore rimless eyeglasses*
> *which allowed a full view*
> *of her face.   In the mornings,*
> *her blonde hair fell in waves*
> *around her face as though she*
> *had used a hundred wave clips*
> *in the night.*
> *For work, she pulled her long*
> *hair back, tight against her head*
> *like a stocking cap, then twisted*
> *it into a smooth knot she called*
> *a chignon.*

My mother was proud when she
earned an office at the local newspaper.

Broad shouldered, and in heels
as tall as many of the men,
she smiled each day as she walked
past their desks to her glass
enclosed office where she
operated the new Fairchild
machine used for the
wireless transfer of photos.

I was happy for her, but as for me,
I didn't care about new technology.
I liked the weekends when
she heated a thin layer of oil
in her black, cast iron frying pan,
cut thick slices of sweet potatoes
and slowly turned the slices,
seasoning them with salt
and pepper, sugar and cinnamon,
or whatever was close by.

When my mother was cooking,
she seemed quite ordinary.

Kayla Conway

You Live in Hopes

She could hear the peepers far away in their mud holes. Their song, like a dirge slicing through the hazy dark, calling in an impossible rain. The air was thick. Callie counted the seconds between each roll of thunder, rumbling like a low growl on the other side of the mountain. The cicadas' buzz rose and fell, fading on the odd breeze. It stirred Callie's hair, lifting rogue wisps away from her damp forehead. To her it seemed like night trapped in all the heat from the day and kept it, waiting to wrap it around bodies in the dark. A gash opened across the sky as heat lightning lit up the clouds. You can see the edge of Heaven, Callie thought. She opened her legs, unsticking her thighs from each other, and sprawled across the bed. Callie stretched like she had when she was trying to grow, pushing her arms and legs way out, grabbing for each corner of the bed from the middle. She couldn't reach. She was restless.

"I'm going for a walk, Daddy."

What she'd said echoed in her head. She turned over again, her mind racing. The room began to smother her and she inched closer to the open window her bed bordered. She let the gauzy curtains, now stirring, dance over her bare arms. Callie counted the freckles on her forearm, dark from the sun but now pale in the last of the moonlight. She counted forty-one before the moon slipped behind a cloud that looked like a moving chunk of the sky. Callie moved her hands to her stomach and felt its flatness beneath her palms. Inhaling sharply, she gathered all her air and let it settle in her belly. It expanded. Lifting her linen gown, it protruded from her frame. This is what she would look like. This is what was coming.

A wave of nausea hit her. She stumbled out of her room and ran to the slop bucket beside the stove. She tasted sick in her throat and let it roll from deep inside her. The rain started slow, rhythmically, and then dropped all at once. Callie heaved as the first clap of thunder trapped itself between the valley's stone walls. Through watery eyes, she stared into the bucket. The half chewed sorghum biscuit she'd stole off the stove after supper floated around with bits of old fatback. She watched her food swim in the pail as the smell of dry earth, its thirst finally whet, and vomit, hit her nose.

All she tasted was guilt.

Callie Blanche Watts

"I see you girl."

It was the first thing he'd ever said to her. She remembered her cheeks growing hot with his words. She remembered being glad her face looked heat-stroked from the stove as to cover her blush. She'd heard that voice before, shouting orders to men, telling a dirty joke that made the men look her way; but never had it spoke to her. She looked up at the voice's owner, the man standing in front of her, burning holes in her with his stare.

All the men in the camp looked the same to Callie. As long as she could recall, they'd always been dirty, weary, and breathless from razing the hills, her daddy included. Yet they had a strange peace about them like they knew they were working to meet one end: the mountain would kill them for killing it. The mountain hadn't killed Callie's daddy though. Her mama'd say that life wasn't that kind. He was basically dead; the widow-maker that crushed him had made him a cripple, breaking the promise its name suggested. All he'd do was sit and stare, his blank eyes fixed on the willow in the lower yard, right by the creek bed that ran through it. But Callie swore when she'd whisper to him, his eyes were alive.

When she was small, Callie imagined that her daddy was

getting all his life's sleep in one go with his eyes open, or that he was just thinking awfully hard about something. He'd do small things, as time passed, eventually coming to lift his own spoon to his mouth, still missing the hole half the time. Despite this, she'd picture his head's insides, sharp as ever, counting each blade of grass by eyeballing or every vein in the potted fern Mama'd sat on his windowsill. Mostly, she'd imagine him on a grand quest to speak again. To meet God and tell him to send Callie a message, answering all her childish secrets.

"I broke Mama's vase," or "I saw brother kill that red bird, but I didn't tell nobody but you."

Now she wondered what he'd send God to say to her when she whispered that name into his ear: Walt Coffey.

Walt's look matched his voice. He was a sturdy man, broad shouldered. His dark hair was slicked the way men wore it on the pomade cans. She didn't think much of him except that he tried too hard to impress the few girls besides Callie in Loving Branch. But for all his trying, he didn't seem to catch not a one. The first time she'd seen him was on her way to the cook camp with Mama. His backed was turned to them as they'd walked past. He was working on rigging, pulling chains tight around the trunk of a recently felled spruce, ready to be dragged away. His suspenders were drawn over his bare shoulders, red and wet with the early sun. The muscles in his back rippled beneath his skin, the same way you could see each sinew in a horse's leg, or a dog's, kicking in its sleep.

She'd heard men mention him. They'd quiet down when she drew near, picking up plates, despite having turned grown in the camp and accustomed to their roughness.

"Strong as hell and mean to boot; he's got a quiet way 'bout him. You better watch your girls, Stewart. That boy's got a face on him," one had said before noticing her hovering around their table, wiping down the next one over in long circles.

It always seemed funny to Callie that you could never have

seen somebody your whole life, but once you did, you'd never stop seeing them as long as you lived. So it was with Walt. She had tried to ask her mama about him, slipping her question into their quiet conversation over whether to cook up taters or pintos for the men's dinnertime.

"Mama? Who's that new foreman? Is he one of the Coffey boys from out near the fork?" she asked softly, trying to seem nonchalant. She watched her mama squash a tiny piss ant with her thumb as it crossed her cutting block before she answered.

"Why?" her voice was flat. "Have you finally decided to do what those old biddies down at the church keep whispering about and get yourself a man? Cause Lord forbid, you can't live no other way." She exaggerated her accent with her last lines. Callie's mama had never made any effort to hide her true feelings about being stuck in the Branch. She was always brutally honest about throwing away her chance at an education for what was once love and then that first baby nobody talked about.

"No," she answered firmly. "I was just asking since he practically owns us now."

"Nobody owns you, Callie Blanche. You do well to remember that." Her mama had said those words with such conviction Callie silenced herself immediately, and they returned to their slow work, paying not one to Walt Coffey.

Having been surrounded by men either too old or too stupid to care about her whole girlhood, Callie had always been content to be alone, and happily skipped any mooncalf phase. She'd fill her time walking into the bush behind the hog pen, and melting slowly into the hills for hours, her back disappearing into the cool shadow of the pine. She'd walk the creek, sometimes stepping into it, her bare toes curling at its cold. No matter the time of year or Mama's threats of sickness, she'd tuck her dress up into her waistband and expose her whole leg to the trees. Her thighs were dark where they should have been milky. Callie wasn't about covering up when there was no one to see her. Sometimes her brother would walk with her, but he was too stuck in his head and hung up on one of the Stewart girls that he didn't care either way. After walking through speckled sun, she'd reach a clearing and see the spring. The rocks sloped down on both sides to catch the water Callie mistook for nectar in her own mind. As far as she was concerned, she was swimming in God's wash basin. Maybe if she floated long enough he'd scoop her up and carry her away.

When she was alone, she'd strip down to her slip and slowly dip herself into its sunbaked water, letting it froth around her body. On hot days she'd jump in naked as a jay bird and swim to the bottom where the water was cold. In the unnatural heat they'd gotten so early she'd been doing it enough. Oftentimes, though, she'd just float on her back and let the water lay over her, hugging her breasts and licking her thighs.

It was there that she'd let the quiet sink deep in her bones. She'd float there, drunk off the sickly syrup smell of the fresh bloomed sweet bubbies and think of everything. Naturally, she'd mull over what troubled her and for days it had only been one thing, one person. Callie couldn't shake the heavy pain in her chest when she'd see Walt working. She'd feel his eyes on her and sometimes their gazes would meet. His dark eyes would pierce her own for a second, but then Callie would remember herself, break the gaze, and break the veil laying over her eyes. He'd say nothing to her when he'd take his tray from her hands. A nod from him was all she'd get as he took his food and went off to sit in the far corner of the mess tent, brooding over God only knew what. Seventeen years Callie had loved the creek, and the trees, and the quiet, and even her crippled daddy and cold mama more than any boy. But Walt Coffey was a man.

She didn't know what to say when his voice growled those words softly at her. "I see you girl," echoed across eternity in her mind. It seemed as if it'd taken Callie her whole life to answer him. All those feelings of disgust and interest and fear of him bubbled up in her.

"I see you, *boy.*"

She'd said it, and she could never take it back.

Walt Coffey

"I see you girl."

That was the first thing he'd said to the girl in the kitchen. Callie Blanche Watts. He supposed she went by plain Callie, but hadn't had the chance to call her by it. He'd been watching her since he'd got to the camp. He'd stare at her as she stood over the hot stove, wisps of hair breaking from her plait and sticking to her forehead. He couldn't read her. He didn't even know how old she was. The distance from the line to his bench at the far end of the mess tent served as far enough to lose sense. She seemed quiet and cold, almost aloof, like her mama. He'd seen men give her winks, tell her she was pretty despite her being what most called plain. She met each advance with a hard stare. She didn't need to speak for them to know they'd just been sent to Hell. Beads of sweat gathered at her hairline. Her brow furrowed with concentration as she stirred the pot. He wondered what she smelled like in a lather. Walt bet her sweat smelled sweet, like lemongrass or something women bought in secret and later attributed to feminine charm.

Walt had first seen her from the road. He remembered passing a small gray house. The chimney had been pouring smoke, despite the heat of the morning sun, and the inside was dark. He'd seen a figure sitting in a window, still and dark. Someone was hanging sheets on the line, the linens fresh from a dip in the creek. The woman hung the sheets with care; he recognized her as Evelyn Watts, their cook woman. He had heard her yell, but he didn't know who at. He backtracked so he could see where the yard touched the woods. The form of a girl slipped into the woods, her light blue dress speckled with sunlight. Something about that girl caught him. He hadn't recalled the last time he'd been to church, so he'd stopped his trek to town and cut into the woods at his first chance.

He'd followed all he could see of her for what had seemed like an aeon. The only glimpses he caught of her were blue gingham. She moved like she'd lived as long as the mountains themselves, gliding in between rhododendrons. Walt watched silently as she stepped into the creek bed. He didn't expect her to, the season had arrived early, and with it the heat, but not enough to go in like that. Never mind his doubts though, she'd rolled her dress up into its waist and walked slowly in the cold water. Every now and then she'd stoop and pick up a piece of quartz and stare at it intently. He'd still hadn't seen her face, just her back and sun darkened legs. They finally reached a clearing, the sunlight blinding him and the sound of water filling his ears. He'd found a boulder and stood behind it, craning to see if she'd turn around. He remembered his breath growing shallow when he saw her bare back, the dress sliding off in one motion. She'd slipped into the pool slowly, testing the water, and then submerged her whole body. She dove deep and came to the surface, ending up on her back. She floated in the clear water, surrounded by flecks of mountain gold in the shallows. He finally saw her face. It was calm and her eyes were closed. She looked otherworldly with the way the water made long patterns on her naked skin and her freckles caught water droplets, covering her face in jewels. He thought for a second about reaching out, jumping in, taking her. She'd have to want him. He'd seen her.

***

Her hair smelled like cotton when he took her. Like fresh pressed sheets. Too clean. He didn't look in her eyes when he pushed himself inside her. It was strange how easy he had laid her down. He'd only had to press his face into hers, leading her to the ground. Walt felt the earth give slightly beneath their weight and Callie's body sink into the clay. The creek gurgled to his right, making the only noise in the dark. The curtain the willow draped around them seemed to block out the night noises. The frogs were silent; maybe they were watching him. Walt tried to find his rhythm, hoping he didn't embarrass himself like when he was alone. He could feel a wetness on his cheek when his face brushed hers, but she remained silent beneath him. Walt felt like a man. He had all the power being foreman was supposed to mean. She had thrown herself at him, following him out into the dark. He'd heard her say something to that cripple of a daddy she had. He was glad of it now, that no father would run out loosing buckshot into the bushes at the man having his daughter. He looked at Callie, laying in the soft ground under his heavy frame. She looked peaceful, like she had gotten her wish. "You want this," he hissed into her hair. His voice had lost any of the softness he had used to lure her out of the house. Time passed slowly and the quiet made it seem like they were both suspended in a joined sleep, a dance only he knew. He pressed his face deeper into her hair. The smell reminding him again of laundry on the line.

He thought of his mama, carefully pinning up quilts to sun. Clothes pins stuck out of her mouth like funny teeth. He remembered running between them, watching as the sun filtered through in reds and blues onto his young skin. Walt would bury his face far into the basking fabric. If he breathed deep enough, he could smell the starch. He could smell the water and even his mama's hands, dry and cracked from scrubbing, scrubbing, scrubbing, on the washboard all morning. His mama would watch him with a mournful look as his dirty hands touched each strip of precisely stitched fabric. Calicos, flannel, gingham, all arranged in granny squares. Each patch seemed a tiny world, a new pattern completely different from its neighbor. The wash day he remembered most came into his head as he tried to pace himself. Callie had gone limp beneath him. He let his thoughts return to that day. He saw and heard it all: Mama's yell to bring in the quilts before the rain, her face when Walt ripped her favorite one off the line, letting it fall into the fresh mud, her quiet hate of her son in that moment and forever after, and his own smile at what he'd just done.

He finished quickly, letting out a groan. Having sown his seed, he got up and brushed dirt from his knees. Callie was quiet, her eyes staring up into the willow's branches. Before he left he brushed a strand of hair from her face and picked a leaf from her skin, tenderly, carefully. He'd done what he'd come to do. Walt pushed off the ground with one hand and stood up over Callie. He saw that the thighs he'd just been between were streaked with blood and dirt and that their romp had torn the hem of Callie's dress. Her breasts rose up and down in weak breaths from beneath her satin slip. He turned to leave. Walt let his gaze rest on her face one last time and met eyes with Callie. They locked with his and the fierce green he'd seen before looked gray and dull in the dim light. It struck him that the Callie he'd thought about and watched and been denied by and whispered to in the dark was gone and all that was left were those hollow eyes. Women had a strange way about virtue. Callie needed time to herself to realize what she'd given him. But as he walked away he realized he didn't care about Callie Blanche Watts. He parted the curtain of willow leaves and left her on the ground. He skirted the trees, avoiding the light that streamed from the small house and stopped right before the tree line. Walt reached the road silently. As he began to walk he turned his head skyward and started counting stars, an old habit when alone in the night. Something stopped him: a cry, a weak moan like a kitten calling for the teat. He stopped and strained his ears to hear the sound again. He heard nothing. Night always filled people with odd thoughts and evil ways.

Sam Barbee

Godhead

A snowstorm carols, comes a hundred-nights wide.
Beamless, still bright, encasing every dark note.

False-deities slur our intimacies with brittle edicts.
They pose in costumes of caring, awash in remedies.

By morning, snowfall has christened our pasture in white.
We receive this indenture.

Even quiet happens fast now . . .
silence attempts to scribble joy into this likeness.

Milestones and benchmarks covered by flurries.
We lie back, embrace, recall once-green idioms.

The meadow stream shimmers along the treeline.
Surges escape beneath gleam.

Splotched goats kneel at the pond before their water-god
and observe inborn rituals as they sup.

Janis Harrington

Groundhog Day

Three weeks after Robert's death, I risk
a modest celebration: birthday cake
and small gifts—socks, hand cream, book—
soberly wrapped. No effusive card.
No streamers or balloons. No guests.
Overhead, slow footsteps thud
a path from her bedroom's curtained gloom.
I strike a match, hoping to lift our spirits,
spark a time-out from our sorrow.
Frozen at the threshold, she stares,
pain in her blue eyes, then reproach. Too soon
for rites of the living. Candles' temporal flare
cannot dispel his spectral shadow.
Wordless, she retreats to grief's burrow.

Peggy Ann Tartt

Mad Love

This morning before it rained,
before the teapot whistled *ready,*

I wandered the streets of the past
again in my mind to the place

where father, whom I never truly
got to know, had made a new life

for himself with a woman
he must have loved madly

because he left us for her
all those years ago.

                    Much of life
is like that, is crazily magnetic,

is the looking in from the outside
and longing for the perceived difference.

For what else could pull a man
away from one family to another

if not mad love? Like a birder
drawn deep into a woods

to glimpse the rareness of a bird,
its peculiar song or feathers.

When he died,
there were no revelations,

no pigeons alighted on my windowsill—
an augury that superstitious kin

believes is a sign of death.
And because I barely knew him,

I felt only a draft of indifference
along the nape of my neck.

Had he returned at times with purpose
like perennials or even like dreams,

he would have grown on us and,
little by little, I would have learned

to forgive him his absences—
*Quia nesciunt quid faciunt.**

[*For they know not what they do.]

136 *Peggy Ann Tartt*

Margaret Montet

Form 1040A

This memento is a strange one. I don't know where to put it other than a plastic sleeve to preserve the brittle paper on which it is printed. It's my parents' United States tax return from 1963, showing both my sister and me as dependents. This is probably the only year we would both be listed, since around the time this form would be submitted, she would be quitting nursing school, going to secretarial school, and then work, marriage, family, etc. I have a 'B' after my name on this form because I was born that year.

There's another dependent, sort of, listed on this form. Feminists, hold onto your hats. My mother's Social Security number is listed under my father's, and under the tiny print: "Wife's number if joint return." My mother's name is nowhere on the form and the instructions are directed at the man filling it out. Halfway down the page, the instructions tell the citizen to claim exemptions under this heading: "EXEMPTIONS FOR YOURSELF—AND WIFE." I want to make a stink about this chauvinist wife-slighting business until I realize that my mother was a homemaker, had no income, and saw my father as head of the household. Instead I'll say, Oh how quaint, and I'm glad the form was changed by the time I began paying taxes as a single.

My only sister, Audrey, was 17 ½ years older than me and had to suffer the indignity of informing her high school friends that her mother was pregnant. That's the way I imagined it, anyway, that my sister suffered this humiliation because I chose that year to appear rather than any of the previous seventeen years. Although she was always kind to me, I imagined that she resented my appearance because I took the attention away from her, the formerly only child. My mother told the story about when my parents were getting ready to brave the late-March icy roads to go to the hospital to await my arrival. Audrey was sleeping, and responded in a breathy, half-asleep voice, "Okay, I'll see you tomorrow." There's a black-and-white picture of her with her teased 1960s dark brown hair and white button-front shirt, standing on our porch at the Cape May house holding the bundle of joy—brand new me—and she's not smiling. What was I to think?

I remember her trimming my fingernails when I was really little, and teaching me how to float on my back in the ocean. She took me to the beach a lot and we'd rent a raft to float or ride the waves in. I still go to that same spot on the beach where we went. It was known as Steger's Beach then because that family owned the beach supply store across Beach Avenue, and also ran the on-sand concession where beachgoers could rent chairs, umbrellas, and rafts, and buy cold soft drinks. There was a clock on top of the store which is still there even though the stores under it have changed.

Audrey also took me to see K.C. and the Sunshine Band (my favorite band then) at Great Adventure (now Six Flags), and we stayed for two shows. K.C. wore an orange sequined polyester jumpsuit for the early show and a blue sequined jumpsuit for the later. The many photographs I shot with my pocket instamatic camera aid my memory of this. She took me to see Saturday Night Fever before I was old enough, because she wanted to see it and no one else in our family was interested, not even my brother-in-law. I don't know how she pulled that off.

For all my young life, my mother had me convinced that my sister was a paragon of virtue and an angelic figure to look up to. Aside from quitting nursing school after my parents put out the money for tuition, room & board, textbooks, and uniforms, everything my sister did was held up as a model for me. It was a template to follow. When I got ready to leave for college, that nursing school story was used as a cautionary tale over and over. "Don't quit!" "Whatever you do, don't quit," my mother said. I didn't quit, but I transferred, and then hung around to get a master's degree.

Once I was an adult, I found out my sister was not a paragon or an angel, but a regular kid who took risks and might have gotten into the occasional predicament. She told me she liked to go to parties and came home tipsy more than once. She didn't think Mommy noticed, "but Daddy probably did because he used to be on those ships with all those young guys." She told me that the nursing school was run by strict nuns who would walk by the dorm rooms in the evening to make sure you were sitting up straight in your desk chair studying. You could go on dates, but not many did because you needed special dispensation from the Pope or the top nun or something. There's a flip side to every story, and this is the flip side to my mother's cautionary tale.

I suppose my mother figured that since they were older parents (she was 40 and he was 48 on that cold night in March 1963 when I was born) that Audrey's growing-up experience would be more relatable to me than their own. That strategy might have some merit, but as a late-in-life "surprise child," I had the unique experience of being raised in the 1950s even though it was the 1970s.

And about that "surprise child" business: though the 1963 1040A doesn't show it, my father retired from the U.S. Coast Guard around the time of my birth. He had thought they'd live a quiet life at their seashore home in Cape May and he would buy a boat. Because of me he had to go back to work and we moved to Staten Island and then Central New Jersey where the United States Department of Agriculture jobs were. They kept the Cape May house which my sister and I share now. They dreamed of going back there but didn't until I was away at college. I thrived in high school marching band and they didn't want to wreck that. I was SO shy. When they did move back, my father was disabled from a stroke and my mother spent most of her time taking care of him. I always felt guilty for wrecking their first retirement (USCG), but on the occasion of his second retirement (USDA), his work buddies told me how he used to brag about me and my good grades and my music endeavors. He did? Huh.

Later into my adult life, when I caught up with my Chicagoan cousin, also Margaret, she told me about their visit the year Mommy was pregnant. "They were so excited, and discussing boy and girl names. Your father wanted you to be Margaret Mary even though my parents already named me that." And it's true, until she got married and took her husband's name, there were two MMMs in the world.

The biggest justification for my existence came during a conversation with my sister. I don't remember where this revelation took place, but it might have been that fabulous river cruise on the Danube or the road trip to Concord, Massachusetts. It could have been on the telephone or at a family gathering. I don't remember. I asked Audrey how awful it was to be blessed with a baby sister at age 17. She said, to my surprise and unexpected delight, that she thought it was great. Finally, she explained, their stifling attention would be taken off her because they had a baby to deal with. They did dote on me, until I was eight and the first of Audrey's children arrived. Grandchildren!

I love looking at that form. The simplicity of it contrasts with the complex tax procedure I pay someone to take care of today. I like the old-timey font the government used, and my father's barely-legible handwriting. He made his 'e's like I do, like backwards 3s, and I never realized that. The one-sided 1040A makes us look like a typical family with two kids, but there are so many stories, imaginations, and memories beyond those words on the brittle paper.

Joanne Durham

DECEMBER

You shrink happiness
to fit inside the possibilities.
Attached to three tubes and an IV,
eating jello and consommé for dinner,
the sound of your wife's voice
is the width of pleasure.

We crowd into this new definition,
gathering close
to your flickering fire,
which, barely moving,
casts giant shadows
against the hospital walls.

Wedged between
the sliding curtains
and memories of easier times,
your spirit clings
to each remaining crevice
of your diminishing room.

Peter Verbica

A Wish for Earth

A flyover over Pluto
made me solemn

-- not because of the cold,
desolation,
or dead silence of space --

but because of the
pockmarks created by meteors.

Some people are like that,
I thought.
No atmosphere to burn up
the bombardment of
information
as it hits the surface
of the soul.

I am Pluto, I realize,
thinking,

what life would be like
if I was Earth.

And I could stop drinking.

Elise Wallace

A Tribute to (My Mother's) Breasts

I look down at my own two breasts and wonder if they look will ever look like hers. Hers are rounder, more full and get the attention from boys that I never have experienced but I'm not sure how to handle those looks and comments. We're in the same grade as in middle school but she looks much older with her mascara, tight jeans and painted nails. Her name is Alex, which is another point of envy. It's a cool name that sets her apart from other girls with regular girl names. It's only cool for Alex because when you look at her, you'd never mistake her for a boy.

My best friend and I found white v-neck T-shirts at a department store in the mall. The material was cheap linen and too thin to wear on its own. The fabric didn't hang, it clung to your body, no matter the size. I bought a medium, afraid that the small would fit too tightly and indicate I wanted my body to be noticed. My friend bought a small. She was a thinly built dancer who wore a bra size almost identical to mine. She couldn't understand why I bought a medium. I brushed off her frustration. I am and was then, most definitely a size small. On the day I was born my grandfather special ordered an outfit for me to wear home. The store didn't have anything small enough for a premature, four-pound baby.

I knew my boobs wouldn't get very large, but I hoped. I knew based on my mother's breasts that mine weren't going to get to the sensuously-weighted, rounded size I saw everywhere: Commercials, TV shows, magazine ads, women on the street with corset-style halter tops. Alex walking down the middle school hallway with highlighted hair and earrings that jingled.

My mother never minded when I walked into her bathroom to ask a question or have a conversation. I sat on the side of the jacuzzi tub while she got ready. Her sink was on the left, closest to the white shuttered windows that traversed the entire corner of the bathroom. Hers was the first female body I saw in full. Her breasts always looked small compared to her powerful thighs and two-children hips.

I started folding layers of toilet paper squares to place in my training bra. I pulled five squares off the roll and folded them carefully back and forth along the perforated edges. The square was placed in a diamond orientation over my nipple. That way the straight line of the sides wouldn't be evident at the top of my breast where my shirts hung closest to my chest. The soft toilet paper faded away gently to create a subtle, rounded effect.

One of the earliest memories of my mother's chest involves salt water. The oceanic saline solution stung my eyes. I was traumatized by a year that my father had held my hand down the beach and a wave crashed my small body into the sand, dousing me in salt water. I came up crying and sputtering sand and salt.

The four of us, mom, dad, and sister, waded out to the ocean, fighting waves, screaming at the cold water making its way up our warm, lotion-covered bodies. When a large wave, too tall for us to avoid, crashed over me, I made my way over to my mother as best I could through squinted eyes and droplets of salt water. I wiped my eyes on the fabric over her soft, pliant breasts. The foam pads in her bathing suits soaked up the excess water and grit.

Her nipples were bigger than mine. Even though it's been years since I've walked in on my mother after a shower, I remember that. Darker too.

The night before her surgery we compared our breasts. She let me touch. Ours are the same size. Enough for you to hold completely in your hand. That's always the response I receive from lovers when I comment on the small-size of my breasts. They like that they can hold them in their hands.

I asked her if she'd said goodbye to them — any poem, or ritual. She told me that she'd been talking to them. The night before she had asked my father, her husband, and the only lover to hold her body, she asked him to kiss them goodbye.

I wondered if that was a tearful moment. Had she cried? Did he? Do goodbye kisses to breasts lead to making love?

She was diagnosed with cancer before I left for a five month trip backpacking trip that would keep me away from home. Six weeks into my trip I came home the night before her surgery. My mother, father and I sat on the back porch on wicker couches. They sat on either end of the long couch and I curled up on the adjacent love seat. She told me that she was relying on the people in her life and didn't need to see a therapist. It was a genuine remark and I could see that she received the space and time to process this decision from my father and from her friends.

She was scheduled for a double mastectomy and the first stages of reconstruction.

While she spoke somewhat tearfully, my father reached across the top of the couch cushion and brought her hand to his lips. It was the only time I've seen him kiss her so tenderly, and the only time I've seen him kiss anything besides her readily-puckered lips.

The next morning, while my parents attended appointments, pre-op procedures and while the medical staff put my mother under anesthesia I was out running errands.

In between dropping off my camera film at the drugstore and buying a bottle of wine for a dinner date with a hometown romantic interest, I stopped to buy a bra. Earlier that day I'd seen my date and he'd commented that I was still wearing the cheap Walmart bra I'd bought for my travels despite being home and amongst my clothes and belongings. It wasn't meant as a slight, but I wanted to feel beautiful and presentable that evening. I wasn't able to find my more attractive bras in the boxes of my stored belongings. I thought I'd buy a cheap black bra for the evening.

Walking the aisles I looked up to find the sign, INTIMATES. I was looking specifically for a bralette. Years ago I'd decided to stop wearing bras with padding and underwire. Even though the most flattering bra I'd owned had underwire, gel pads and a front clip. Wearing that piece gave me the closest thing to cleavage I could ever claim.

I daydreamed about having larger breasts. When I explored my own body I began to realize that breasts were an integral part of my state of arousal. When I discovered porn I looked for women with a generous, bouncy chest. Larger breasts became a preference of mine more than my partners.

I made my way between rows of hanger-clipped bras. Every single one was padded. I slid aside hangers with a plastic, grinding click and pressed my fingers to the softly molded cups. Foamy circles inserted in every single one. Knowing I would be returning to my travels shortly, and that my date did not truly care, I walked out of the store empty-handed. I had to pick up wine and it was close to the end of my mom's surgery.

When I walked into the hospital lobby the receptionist was on the phone and the security officer did not look up to offer herself as a source of information. I looked to the walls and saw large framed photographs of places that I had visited during my travels. Green mountains, fading into wispy blue ridges. They were familiar scenes, but the colors were overly saturated and mocking. I had just been there, in those places faraway. I carried everything on my back to survive out there and now I was here. I headed to the elevators which moved so slowly but I thought this was because it was a hospital. Elevators shouldn't move too quickly and jostle a post-op patient or shock a newborn baby. A sign said not to use cell phones because of interference with heart monitoring technology.

Mom was awake, but groggy from the pain medication. Dad stood up from the bedside chair and I walked to take his place. I took my mother's hand. She said with relief - it's over, I did good. I told her she did very good. She lifted my hand to her mouth and kissed it with her eyes closed.

There was a slight rise to her chest from the expanders. These would be slowly inflated to stretch her healing skin so the final implants would have a perfectly-sized home. The surgeon came into the room for a friendly followup visit. She was wearing blue scrubs and her highlighted hair was pulled back in a loose ponytail. She was so freckled-tan that I couldn't tell the difference between freckles and skin. This made her eyes more blue and I wondered if she went to a tanning bed, or maybe had a beach house she visited each weekend. I followed the freckles down her v-neck scrub top and saw the lifted strap of her beige bra, held suspended by the weight of her right breast.

I asked what they do with removed breasts. They dig into the tissue and find all the cancer, they biopsy and test. Then most likely, mom said, they incinerate the tissue. That is the most sanitary procedure. Mom asked about the view from the window. I described a few trees, but mostly rooftops and AC units, and a tall pipe that spewed liquid and steam into the air.

Probably the remains of my burned boobs, she said, and laughed.

Four days later her humor was faded by the narcotic painkillers, constipation, fatigue and emotional struggle. Each day was long and the enormity of the process in front of her loomed around every small, quiet moment in the house or on the back porch or during one of our very short walks.

It helped to distract her with other projects, my life, anyone else's life. We sat on her bed and flipped through magazines. I had a suitcase full of fashion mags, old New Yorkers and conservative editorials from my grandparents house. I was working on an art project that used hundreds of small pieces of paper for a collage. Mom flipped through the bright, glossy pages and asked me about colors and textures. When I nodded she ripped out the page and placed it next to me.

She stopped on one page. Those are breast implants, she said. The picture showed two manicured hands with red painted nails and bulky silver bracelets each holding a clear, round pouch of fluid. You could see the red nail polish through the implants, watery and out of focus.

I asked if those were filled with silicone and leaned into the page. The caption offered no helpful information. Mom told me that older implants, some still today, are filled with a saline solution. Salt and water. Most women choose silicone because it feels more realistic but saline filled implants are still used. Her expanders will be filled with saline by the plastic surgeon until they are the right size for her implants.

The article discussed the technology, historical issues and current trends with breast implants. These implants, though were for enhancement, aesthetics, ego, not for cancer survivors. Active cancer patients. We guessed that in the future regenerative medicine would be able to grow real breasts, tissue and cells, and then attach to cancer patients. Eventually this technology will become so commonplace that luxury will walk in and models will have home-grown breasts too.

She ripped out the page.

It was late, almost ten o'clock and the house was quiet. My mother lay on her back, the only way she was allowed to during recovery. She unzipped her jacket. Underneath was the post-op bra cinched tight with hook-eyes, meant to hold everything in place. There were drain bags for recovery fluid and tubes that were choked beneath the elastic and cotton of the bra. She complained about these tubes. She was a certified RN in the ICU and ED before she was a mother. She knows exactly what small, foam piece she would have fit onto each to those tubes, so it didn't irritate her skin, and pinch and itch. If she had been in that OR she would have put those on each tube.

Maybe she does this every night, or in the middle of the afternoon while I'm away, but I've never seen it until this moment. She unhooks each eyelet and sighs with the release. She moves aside the tubes and drain bags. Her body is bare and exposed from the chest up. She moves her fingers lightly over the tape along the bottom of two white squares placed over her chest, not in a diamond orientation, but plan and square and taped tightly. She sighs, enjoying her ability to itch every so slightly her skin with nerves still waking up.

She is so comfortable, half-naked on the bed. A level of ease that doesn't come with exposing two breasts, real breasts with nipples and hair follicles and sagging weight. She closes her eyes and begins to drift off. I take the picture of two silicone breasts held by red-tipped lady hands and cut it up into small pieces.

Contributors

Sam Anderson: Sam lives at the edge of Omaha, Nebraska with his wife and two sons. He earned his BFA from the University of Nebraska at Omaha, and his MFA from Minnesota State University, Mankato. He writes about the commonplace spaces in rural and suburban Americana, and often seeks to unveil the darker nature lurking just beyond the surfaces. His work has appeared in such places as *Fine Lines magazine, NEBRASKAland magazine, Microfiction Mondays Magazine*, and *The Gambler Magazine*.

Sam Barbee: Sam's poems have appeared *Poetry South, The NC Literary Review, Crucible, Asheville Poetry Review, The Southern Poetry Anthology VII: North Carolina, Georgia Journal, Main Street Rag*, and *Pembroke Magazine*, among others; plus on-line journals *Vox Poetica, Pyrokinection*, and *The Blue Hour*. His Second poetry collection, *That Rain We Needed* (2016, Press 53), was a nominee for the Roanoke-Chowan Award as one of North Carolina's best poetry collections of 2016. He was awarded an "Emerging Artist's Grant" from the Winston-Salem Arts Council to publish his first collection *Changes of Venue* (Mount Olive Press); has been a featured poet on the North Carolina Public Radio Station WFDD; received the 59th Poet Laureate Award from the North Carolina Poetry Society for his poem *The Blood Watch*; and is a Pushcart nominee.
Sam lives in Winston-Salem with his wife and is the current President of the NC Poetry Society.

Jenny Bates: Jenny is a poet from the foothills of North Carolina and a member of Winston-Salem Writers and NC Poetry Society. She has two published books, *Opening Doors: an equilog of poetry about Donkeys (Lulu Publishing, Raleigh, NC)* and *Coyote with Coffee (Catbird on the Yadkin Press, Tobaccoville, NC)*. Both books reside in the collections of Libraries and Universities (Vanderbilt and the University of Vermont) in the United States and England. Her work has also been published in *Flying South*, Winston-Salem Writers premier literary work. She is a consecutive contributing poet in the Winston-Salem Writers series *Poetry in Plain Sight* and in *2017* she was a top 10 Finalist in the *Press 53 Single Poem Contest*. Her poetry is a reflection of her philosophy of life: *All humans have learned about being human by what we have gained from observing our fellow animals. With a much* *longer history than humans, animals have learned perhaps not to accept, but to respect their differences.* Jenny's newest work to be published has appeared in the Fall Issue 2017, Spring 2018 of *laJoie*, a quarterly publication of Animals' Peace Garden, dedicated to promoting appreciation for all beings. All profits donated to animal and Earth-supportive organizations. Published 2018 in *Wild Goose Poetry Review*. Jenny currently volunteers as animal whisperer and helping hand at Plum Granny Farm. An organic local farm in Stokes County, North Carolina.

Gerard Berry: Gerard lives in Winston-Salem, NC, where he has been a physician assistant (P.A.) for 35 years. He currently works with adults at a primary care free clinic and at an addiction medicine center. Gerard and his wife Diana have five adult children. He writes memoir, poetry and short fiction.

Michael Boccardo: Michael's poems have been published in various journals, including *Kestrel*, *Mid-American Review*, *Iron Horse Literary Review*, *The Southern Review*, *Border Crossing*, *Prairie Schooner*, *Nimrod*, *Comstock Review*, and *Best New Poets*, as well as the anthologies *Spaces Between Us: Poetry, Prose, and Art on HIV/AIDS* and *Southern Poetry Anthology, VII: North Carolina*. He is a Pushcart nominee, a past recipient of the Dorothy Sargent Rosenberg Prize, and a finalist for the James Wright Poetry Award. Also, he serves as assistant editor for the poetry journal *Cave Wall*. He resides in High Point, NC, with three rambunctious tuxedo cats.

Wyatt Bond: Wyatt graduated with his MFA in Creative Writing from North Carolina State University, in Raleigh, North Carolina. He currently resides in Raleigh with his dog, Virgil Cane.

Joyce Compton Brown: Joyce has published in numerous journals. Her chapbooks are *Bequest* (Finishing Line Press, 2015) and *Singing with Jarred Edges* (Main Street Rag Publishing, 2018), a finalist in the Cathy Smith Bowers Chapbook Contest.

Spencer K. M. Brown: Spencer's stories have been published in *Scalawag*, *Empty Sink*, *Prime Number*, *Change Seven*, *Flash Fiction Magazine*, and *Unbroken Journal* among others. He was the 2016 Penelope Niven Award for Fiction and was nominated for a 2017 Pushcart Prize for Fiction. He currently lives in King, NC with his beautiful wife, where he is at work on a novel.

Kayla Conway: Kayla is a graduate of Salem College, having received her B.A. in English and Creative Writing in 2017, and is currently pursuing her MLIS at the University of North Carolina at Greensboro. Kayla works full-time as a marketing coordinator but always looks for ways to return to her first love: writing. In her spare time, she enjoys cross-stitching, beefing up on miscellaneous trivia, and watching movies.

Elizabeth Crowell: Elizabeth's work has been published recently in *Sewanee Review*, *Callisto*, *Red Ravina Review*, *The Roanoke Review*, and in *The Saranac Review*. Her essay, *Cancer, So Far*, just won the Bellevue Literary Review contest and her story, *Hunger of the Very Rich* was named a finalist in *Chattahoochee Review*'s Lamar York Fiction Prize. She has a B.A. in English from Smith College and an M.F.A. in Creative Writing/Poetry from Columbia University. She taught high school and college English for many years and currently lives outside Boston with her wife and two children.

Steve Cushman: Steve has published four works of fiction, including the 2004 Novello Literary Award winning novel, *Portisville*, and most recently the novel, *Hopscotch*. His first full-length poetry collection, *How Birds Fly*, is the winner of the 2018 Lena Shull Book Award.

David Dixon: David Dixon is a physician, poet, and musician who lives and practices in the foothills of North Carolina. His poetry has appeared in *LIGHT Journal*, *Rock & Sling*, *The Northern Virginia Review*, *Connecticut River Review*, and elsewhere.

Joanne Durham: Joanne has been reading and writing poetry since childhood. As an elementary teacher she shared the pleasure and power of poetry with her students, and as a reading/language arts supervisor and literacy consultant, has supported teachers in unlocking the joys of poetry as well. Her poems about teaching have been published in *Language Arts* and *The Journal of Reading Recovery*. She feels incredibly lucky to currently live in Kure Beach, NC, where she can write, read, and discover through poetry every day.

Grace Ellis: Grace, the leader of the Winston-Salem Writers Script Group, has seen over two dozen of her plays performed in school auditoriums, churches, parks, orchards, and occasionally in theaters. Grace also writes poems and creative non-fiction. She wrote the original version of "Out in the Yard" as a response to a prompt from Peggy Millin.

Diana Engel: Diana Engel delights in helping others discover their inner poets, in bringing writers and artists together to learn from one another, spark synergy and build the creative community. Her verse has appeared in *Asheville Poetry Review, snapdragon, Greensboro's Visual Poetry Walk, Wild Goose Poetry Review, Perspectives, Open to Interpretation, The Gathering, Wordworks,* and *fire & chocolate.* She served as editor and head of poetry anthology projects for Writers' Group of the Triad and Penn-Griffin Middle School resulting in the anthologies *fire & chocolate* and *Sharing the Light.*

Michael Gaspeny: Michael Gaspeny is the author of *Re-Write Men,* his second chapbook, which appeared in 2017 from Finishing Line Press. His first, *Vocation,* was published in 2013 by Main Street Rag Press. He has won the Randall Jarrell Poetry Prize and the O. Henry Festival Short Story Competition. His poetry has inspired a street sculpture and been posted in shop windows. In his sixteenth year as a hospice volunteer, he has received The (North Carolina) Governor's Award for Volunteer Excellence. A former sportswriter, he covered Arkansas Razorback sports in the 1970s. Retired and living in Greensboro, NC, he taught journalism and English for nearly forty years, mainly at Bennett College and High Point University.

Jonathan Greenhause: Jonathan was the winner of *Aesthetica Magazine's* 2018 Creative Writing Award in Poetry, winner of the 2017 Ledbury Poetry Competition, and a recipient of 3rd Prize in The Plough Poetry Prize 2017. His poems have recently appeared or are forthcoming in *The Carolina Quarterly, december, EVENT, Notre Dame Review,* and *The Sierra Nevada Review,* and his 2nd chapbook *Secret Traits of Everyday Things* was published by Encircle Publications last September. He was also a contributor to last year's *Flying South.*

Allen Guest: Allen is a Senior Lecturer in the Department of Mathematical Sciences at Clemson University, where he currently serves as the course coordinator for multi-variable calculus. He tries to bring the exactness of mathematics to his poetry and hopes his attempt brings a certain clarity of image to his work. Three of his poems have been published in *The Petigru Review* and he has received the following awards: First Place in the 2018 Writers Workshop of Asheville Poetry Contest, Third Place in the 2017 Writers Workshop of Asheville Poetry Contest, Honorable Mention in the 2016 Writers Workshop of Asheville Poetry Contest and a 2019 Pushcart Prize nomination from *The Petigru Review*.

Lucas Hargis: Lucas Hargis is an award-winning visual artist & agented author. He's a fan of mixed metaphors, sacred clowns, mint-chocolate anything, ampersands & fresh perspectives. Growing up as a creative, closeted, trailer park kid in NC, Lucas is an advocate for passionate, voice-y self-expression.

Janis Harrington: Janis' book, *Waiting for the Hurricane*, won the 2017 Lena M. Shull Book Award, sponsored by the North Carolina Poetry Society, and was published by St. Andrews University Press. Three of her poems won awards and appeared in the 2018 edition of *Pinesong*, sponsored by the North Carolina Poetry Society. Her work has also appeared in *Beyond Forgetting: Poetry and Prose about Alzheimer's Disease*, an anthology published by The Kent State University Press; *New Southerner Anthology*; *The Homestead Review*; *Kakalak 2016*; *Off the Coast*; *Midwestern Gothic*; and other journals. She has a Masters degree in English with a Creative Writing focus from North Carolina State University.

Mary Hennessy: A nurse most of her adult life, Mary returned to school late and fell in with a community of generous, word-crazed people. Her poems have appeared in many journals and anthologies. One was nominated for a Pushcart Prize and included in the play *Deployed*. One rode the R-bus line in Raleigh.

JoAnn Hoffman: Jo Ann Steger Hoffman is a writer, editor, and former corporate communications director whose publications include a children's book, short fiction and a variety of poems in literary journals, including *The Merton Quarterly*, *Pinesong*, *New Verse News* and *Ground Fresh Thursday*. She has received recent contest awards from the Carteret Writers, Pamlico Writers and the Palm Beach Poetry Festival. Her 2010 non-fiction book, *Angels Wear Black*, recounts the only technology executive kidnapping to occur in California's Silicon Valley. Ms. Hoffman earned her graduate degree in English and Creative Writing from the University of South Carolina. A native of Toledo, Ohio, she and her husband now live in Cary and Beaufort, North Carolina.

Anthony Howcroft: Anthony's work has been broadly published in a variety of periodicals such as *Writers Magazine USA*, *Words with Jam*, and *The London Magazine*. His stories have also appeared in numerous anthologies and been broadcast on BBC Radio. Originally from Oxford, Anthony now lives in America, where he runs a cognitive computing software company. His first collection, *Nobody Will Ever Love You*, was published in 2015.

Esther Whitman Johnson: Esther is a former high school educator from Southwest Virginia who travels the globe volunteering on five continents, often writing about her journeys. She has completed builds in fifteen countries, ranging from Mongolia to Madagascar, Chile to Cambodia, and points in-between. Her poetry and prose have been published in over two dozen journals and anthologies, most recently *Forgotten Women* and *Black Lives Have Always Mattered*. She is a graduate of the College of William and Mary and holds Masters Degrees in English and Counseling from the University of Virginia.

Michael Kocinski: Michael borrows too many books from the the library at one time; he loves insects; he should have studied etymology in college. He has three children he loves beyond measure and an unflappable wife who is smart, kind, and patient.

Colleen Lanier: Colleen Lanier is a registered nurse with a private consulting firm. She lives in North Carolina, where she works, writes and drinks coffee.

Philip Lawton: First a philosophy teacher and then an investment professional at major insurance companies and international banks, Philip Lawton now writes creative nonfiction. He is a member of Writer House in Charlottesville, Virginia.

Sam Love: Sam is a New Bern, NC writer. He has published numerous nonfiction articles in magazines including *Smithsonian*, and *Washingtonian*.

He has two published novels, *Snap Factor*, and *Electric Honey*. He recently published a poetry book *Cogitation* (Unsolicited Press). His poetry has been published in *Kakalak*, *Slippery Elm*, *Voices on the Wind*, *The Lyricist*, *Flying South* and other publications. His has had six environmental poems in *Eno* published by Duke University. His work has also been featured on Poetry in Plain Sight posters throughout North Carolina. Sam is the author of an award winning illustrated children's book *My Little Plastic Bag* designed to share with children what happens to a plastic bag thrown out of a car window. There is also a Spanish edition *Mi Bolsita Plastica*. Sam's Websites: http://www.samlove.net and www.mylittleplasticbag.com

Barbara Rizza Mellin (cover artist): Barbara is a writer and artist. Her hand-pulled prints and printings have been featured in juried exhibits throughout the U.S. and in one-woman exhibits at Duke U (Durham), Alamance Art Council (Graham), the Hiddenite Arts and Heritage Center, Hiddenite, NC, and Artworks and Red Dog Galleries in Winston Salem, NC. Her work is currently on display at PTI Airport/ Main Terminal in Greensboro, NC. She has been a member of several local and national art groups, including the Printmakers of North Carolina, Women Painters of the Southeast, and Oil Painters of America. She writes frequently about the arts.

Margaret Montet: Margaret writes creative nonfiction that combines place with memoir, music, or culture. She recently earned a Master of Fine Arts Degree in Creative Nonfiction from the Pan European MFA Program at Cedar Crest College. In order to provide herself with food, shelter, and travel money, Margaret works as a librarian at Bucks County Community College sharing her love of research with Pennsylvanians. She teaches Effective Speaking to college students, and she teaches Music History to older adults. Her writing has appeared in such periodicals as *Clever Magazine*, *Pink Pangea*, *Edible Jersey*, *Library Journal*, *America in WWII*, *The Bangalore Review*, and *Danse Macabre*.

Phyllistine Poole: I am a retired librarian and graduate of UNCG, in library information studies. A few of my poems and memoirs have been published in anthologies. I am trying to improve my writing, because like everyone else, I have testimonies that need telling.

156

David Radavich: David's recent poetry collections are *AMERICA BOUND: AN EPIC FOR OUR TIME*, *MIDDLE-EAST MEZZE*, and *THE COUNTRIES WE LIVE IN*. His plays have been performed across the U.S., including six Off-Off-Broadway, and in Europe. He has served as president of the Thomas Wolfe Society, Charlotte Writers' Club, and North Carolina Poetry Society.

Mason Rizzo: Mason does not have a history of published work, though he tries to encase the intersection of his upbringing in the rural south with grief and mourning in his poems to understand his composition as a person.

Peggy Ann Tartt: Peggy authored the poetry volume *Among Bones* (Lotus Pr.), which won the Naomi Long Madgett Poetry Award, and the chapbook *Firestarters* (Mouthfeel Pr.). She is a recipient of several honors, including a Money for Women/Barbara Deming Memorial Fund grant, an Arts & Letters Prize in Poetry, and a Pushcart Prize in Poetry nomination. She has contributed poetry to an array of literary publications, including *Cutthroat: A Journal of the Arts*, *Hospital Drive*, *Margie Review*, *Bryant Literary Review*, *Poem*, *Field*, *Prairie Schooner*, *Pedestal Magazine*, and *Poetry South*. Peggy holds an MFA from the University of Massachusetts-Amherst.

Claire Thomas: Claire currently lives in sunny Southern California, having left Winston-Salem last Fall. She spends her time writing, exploring coffee shops and reading self-help books on the beach.

Peter Venable: Peter has written both free and metric verse for over fifty years. He has been published in *Prairie Messenger*, *Torrid Literature Journal*, *Third Wednesday*, *Windhover - A Journal of Christian Literature* and others. He is a retired clinician, volunteers at a prison camp, seniors' center, and food pantry; and is graced with a happy marriage, daughter, son-in-law, Emma and Yeshua. Visit him at petervenable.com .

Peter Verbica: Peter Coe Verbica grew up on a commercial cattle ranch in Northern California. He obtained a BA and JD from Santa Clara University and an MS from Massachusetts Institute of Technology. He is married and has four daughters.

Donna Love Wallace: Donna lives in Lewisville, North Carolina and is currently director of Poetry In Plain Sight, a Winston Salem Writers' state-wide initiative placing poetry in public spaces. Her poetry appears in *Kakalak 2017*, *The Paddock Review*, *Wild Goose Poetry Review* and *Plainsongs*. Retired from nursing and teaching biblical studies, she rides her bicycle through the foothills and vineyards surrounding her home.

Elise Wallace: Elise is a writer, barista and non-profit arts advocate living in Winston-Salem, NC. This piece is dedicated to her mother, Donna Wallace.

Camilla Wilcox: Camilla lives on a small farm with her husband, Sid Teague, in western Forsyth County. While most of her poetry is centered on their farm life and her observations of nature, her work extends to include observations of her neighbors, who are adjusting to changes in their rural community.

John Sibley Williams: John Sibley Williams is the author of *Disinheritance*, *Controlled Hallucinations*, and the forthcoming Orison Poetry Prize winning *As One Fire Consumes Another*. An eleven-time Pushcart nominee, John is the winner of numerous awards, including the Philip Booth Award, American Literary Review Poetry Contest, Phyllis Smart-Young Prize, The 46er Prize, Nancy D. Hargrove Editors' Prize, Confrontation Poetry Prize, and Vallum Award for Poetry. He serves as editor of *The Inflectionist Review* and works as a literary agent. Previous publishing credits include: *The Yale Review*, *Midwest Quarterly*, *Sycamore Review*, *Prairie Schooner*, *The Massachusetts Review*, *Poet Lore*, *Saranac Review*, *Atlanta Review*, *TriQuarterly*, *Columbia Poetry Review*, *Mid-American Review*, *Poetry Northwest*, *Third Coast*, and various anthologies. He lives in Portland, Oregon.

Sandra Ann Winters: Sandra is the winner of the 2011 Gregory O'Donoghue International Poetry Competition, and a Pushcart nominee, having won numerous poetry awards and commendations in the United States. She is the author of a full-length poetry collection *The Place Where I Left You* (Salmon Poetry 2014), and a chapbook *Calving Under the Moon* (Finishing Line Press 2013). Most recently she has been published in *The Deep Heart's Core, Irish Poets Revisit A Touchstone Poem* (anthology from Dedalus Press, Ireland, 2017), and *Even the Daybreak* (anthology from

Salmon Poetry, 2016). Her poems have been included in the Winston Salem Writers' Poetry in Plain Sight Program, and she has been a featured guest poet in the O Bheal weekly poetry event in Cork City, Ireland.

Katherine Wolfe: Katherine lives in Goldsboro, North Carolina. She is a retired media coordinator with Wayne County Public Schools and a member of the Goldsboro Writers Group. Published works include the memoir *Savannah on My Mind* written with Bettye Clary Toomey and poetry in the *Lyricist, Renaissance, Shoal, Pinesong, Flying South 2017*, and the Winston Salem Writers series *Poetry in Plain Sight*. Her chapbook *Time That Has Gone* will be forthcoming from Finishing Line Press in October.